GOD'S FAVORITE NUMBER

I loved every word I read of *God's Favorite Number*! This is such a timely word for the church in this hour. I highly recommend it to anyone who has a heart to see the Bride become more beautiful for Her Bri␣␣␣␣␣␣␣␣␣␣␣␣␣the lost reached in His name!

uh, Intercessory Prayer Team
low Creek Community Church

If you h␣␣␣␣␣␣␣␣␣␣␣␣inced of the necessity of unity and oneness, you will be after reading *God's Favorite Number*. The author, Ben Peters, masterfully puts together Scriptural illustrations from both the Old and New Testaments showing how important "One" is to God. It is in an atmosphere of unity that God can work and pour out his blessing. Personal illustrations from the author's own life and experience help to make the book both interesting and practical. You will be blessed, encouraged and challenged as you begin to more clearly understand, through reading the book, what is really the "Key To God's Divine Power"

Pastor Robert Smith
West Calgary Full Gospel Church, Calgary, Alberta

This book is a very timely one, as everywhere I go I hear the message of "oneness" with God as well as the need for unity in the body of Christ. I was recently given a song by the Lord called, "One Plus One Is One," not really knowing the depth of what the song was saying until I read Ben's book. It is a message *of* the hour, *for* the hour, and I highly recommend it to all who are seeking to know what is on the mind of God in a very down to earth and relevant way.

JoAnn McFatter,
Prophetic Worship Leader and recording artist,
Kansas City, Missouri

With rich biblical insights, Ben has captured the heart's desire of our heavenly Father. One isn't a lonely number but the only number that brings the unity God desires. This book caused me to take a fresh look at my relationships with other believers.

Randy Demain, Senior Pastor
Amazing Grace Bible Fellowship, Redmond, Oregon

This book is a must for understanding what God is doing in these end times. A great combination of Biblical principles and prophetic visions and revelations. It is Word and Spirit in harmony.

Bill Myers, Senior Pastor
Jubilee Center, Genoa, Illinois

A common quest of pastors, church leaders and Christians everywhere is for revival and growth of the church. The key to having both lies in the pages of this book. Ben Peters has navigated through familiar waters to bring out a simplistic but overlooked truth: Unity must come before revival! For too long, we have tried to bring about revival, while maintaining the walls of our selfish "mini-kingdoms" within the church. It's time for these walls to come down! Do the math: only the devil subtracts and divides. God adds and multiplies. This book brings the clearest revelation I've seen yet of the body of Christ as it should be: as Jesus died for it to be. Every church leader needs to bury him/herself in its pages and be changed. Then shout it from the mountaintops! This book is full of revolutionary revelation. It will pull you into the heart of God and you'll never want to leave!

Scott Schilder, Sr. Pastor
New Life Christian Center
Woodstock, IL

In *God's Favorite Number*, Ben Peters shows us that the revelation of unity in the Church is really the revelation of God's glory. He paints for us a prophetic picture of what that glorious unity looks like, and lays out fresh insights and practical helps on how we can get there. What a joy to realize that God's great harvest is not only to be gathered *in* but gathered *together*!

Jeff Doles, Pastor
Walking Barefoot Ministries
Author, *Healing Scriptures and Prayers*
www.walkingbarefoot.com

GOD'S *Favorite* NUMBER

THE SECRET KEYS AND AWESOME
POWER OF TRUE UNITY

BEN R. PETERS

GOD'S FAVORITE NUMBER

© 2005 by Ben R. Peters

All rights reserved. No part of this publication may be reproduced or transmitted in any form or by any means without permission of the publisher.

ISBN: 0-9767685-0-X

Unless otherwise indicated, Bible quotations are taken from the New King James Version. Copyright © 1983 by Thomas Nelson, Inc. Also: Parts of verses highlighted, underlined or in italics are added by the author for emphasis.

Open Heart Ministries
15648 Bombay Blvd.
S. Beloit, IL 61080
www.ohmint.org
benrpeters@juno.com

CONTENTS

PREFACE

*Y*ou probably have never even considered the fact that God could have a favorite number, and you probably thought that God used the same system of mathematics that works for us here in the earthly realm. But rest assured that God does have a favorite number and His system of mathematics is significantly different than ours.

The fact is that knowing God's favorite number and understanding His system of math is not a trivial matter. The life and power of the church hang on these vital elements of His Kingdom. The truths which we will discuss in this book are not that hard to find in God's eternal Word. They are actually laid out in plain English, Hebrew, Greek, Spanish or any other language which has a reasonably accurate translation of the Bible.

The obvious question is: "Why have we not seen these truths or become aware of their importance and significance?" The answer may be that they are truths which we find hard to reconcile with what has become the norm in Christendom. It is really hard for us to believe that something so contrary to what we have always accepted could be really God's plan and model for His church.

The exciting thing is that God is quickly revealing His passion for His favorite number to His people, the church, His own body, on the earth. And everywhere, His people are learning the power of employing Divine Mathematics on the earth. Keep reading and discover with us just how much God loves His very favorite number and how awesome His Divine Mathematics can be for each of us and for His Kingdom.

CHAPTER 1

SOLVING THE MYSTERY

I love to ask people, especially children, "What do you think is God's favorite number?" The most common answer is seven, then three, and then a variety of other numbers like twelve, five, ten, one and four.

I have never gotten deep into numerology, the study of the significance of different numbers in the Bible. As a student of the Bible, however, I am well aware that certain numbers are used quite often and are considered to have special meanings.

SEVEN

For instance, seven is called the number of perfection or completeness, and it is used quite often in Scripture, 463 times to be precise. To start with, God created a seven day week. He could have made the week ten days or any other number and it would have worked just as well, but He chose seven. Number six represents man, according to the experts, but seven represents God who is complete and perfect.

The church chose seven deacons to handle the practical matter of feeding the widows, etc. Proverbs refers to seven things the Lord hates, seven things that are wonderful on the earth, etc. There were seven churches addressed in Revelation and it could well be that there will be seven millennia in man's pilgrimage on this earth.

Seven is definitely a popular number with God, but is it God's very favorite number? My conclusion is that it is not. It is a number that God appears to favor a lot, but it is not His very favorite number.

THREE

Three is also considered a very significant number. The number three is found 485 times in Scripture. The Trinity, God the Father, God the Son, and God the Holy Spirit, is the most significant use of the number three. But three is also the number of resurrection. On the third day, Jesus arose from the grave. Jesus chose three close friends, Peter, James and John, to pray with Him in the Garden of Gethsemane and to go with Him up the mountain, where He was glorified and visited by Moses and Elijah. As they stood together on the mountain, there were three glorified bodies side by side, with Jesus in the middle. Later, three crosses stood on Mount Calvary, where Jesus died, crucified on the middle cross between two thieves.

The wise men brought three gifts to Jesus; gold, frankincense and myrrh. People deduce from this that there were only three wise men, but that is probably not true. Israel also had three patriarchs; Abraham, Isaac and Jacob.

So, is the number three God's favorite number? Again, I have to say no. It's a great number but not God's favorite. Let's try another one.

TWELVE

Could the number twelve be God's favorite number? This is a number we find many times in both the Old Testament and the New Testament. The number twelve is used a total of 189 times in

Scripture. God gave us twelve months in our calendar year. There were twelve tribes of Israel and twelve disciples chosen by Jesus. Even Ishmael had twelve sons, which God called princes.

Elijah found Elisha plowing with twelve yoke of oxen. Jesus said His Father could send Him twelve legions of angels to deliver Him from the cross. After the multiplying of the loaves and fishes they collected twelve baskets full of leftovers. A woman who came for healing had an issue of blood for twelve years. Twelve is also a popular number in Revelation, with twelve gates of pearl and twelve angels at the gates. The New Jerusalem will be twelve thousand furlongs square. And we could go on and on. But could we say that the number twelve is God's favorite number? I must again say, I'm sorry, but twelve is not God's favorite number.

OTHER POPULAR NUMBERS

The number four is quite common in Scripture (328 times), as is the number five (345 times). There are four directions. There are four New Testament Gospels. Four lepers saved the city of Samaria from starvation. I like the number four. It has always been a favorite number since childhood, but now five is one of my favorite numbers because it is known as the number representing God's grace. I so appreciate His grace and know that I can do nothing without His grace. But neither the number four, nor the number five is God's favorite number. Ten is also a popular number with 249 occurrences, but it is also not God's favorite.

Neither is the number two God's favorite, which surprisingly has more occurrences (835) than any of the other numbers which we have already discussed. God did make two sexes, male and female. He made two lights in the sky to rule the day and the night. He had Noah put two of each animal in the ark. He sent out his disciples two by two. Two angels were stationed in the empty tomb; one at the head and one at the feet. But we cannot say that two is the very favorite number of our eternal God.

GOD'S TRUE FAVORITE NUMBER

To discover what is God's truly favorite number, we can check out Ephesians 1:10, which says,

> *"That in the dispensation of the fullness of times He might gather together in one all things in Christ, both which are in Heaven and which are on earth – in Him."*

When Paul talks about the fullness of times, he is talking about the final end result of all of God's activities in Heaven and earth since creation. He is talking about God's ultimate purpose and plan. So what is His plan? It is to gather everything that exists into one single entity. He wants everything that exists to be contained in His eternal Son, Jesus. **He wants the final number that all creation experiences to be the number one.**

The number one occurs 1969 times in Scripture, more than the totals for the numbers three, four, five, seven and twelve. It is by far the most popular number in all of Scripture.

GOD IS ONE

In addition, it is the only number used by God to identify His very being. For example, the great commandment of Deuteronomy 6 begins with the words,

> *"Hear, Oh Israel; The Lord our God, the Lord is one!"* (Deut. 6:4)

Jesus clearly affirmed this when He declared,

> *" . . . Holy Father, keep through Your name those whom You have given Me, that they may be one as We are."* (John 17:11b)

In this verse, Jesus not only declares that He and His Father are one, but His goal for His disciples is that they also would be one.

Ephesians 4:4-6 uses the number one seven times:

"There is one body and one Spirit, just as you were called in one hope of your calling; one Lord, one faith, one baptism; one God and Father of all, who is above all, and through all, and in you all."

This incredible verse is easy to read through like a poem, but it is important to understand what Paul is trying to say. For instance, there are not many bodies, as we tend to think. We refer to our "local body." That really is not biblical. The local church was never called a "local body." There is only one body. There is only one Spirit. That is, there is only one Holy Spirit. He doesn't teach one group one doctrine and another group a different doctrine. He is in unity with Himself. There is only One of Him and He will not confuse us with different or opposite doctrines.

We could emphasize each of the seven, but the point is clear. In all these things Paul wants us to focus on the fact that God puts things together into one and then all the individual "ones" are also brought into a "oneness."

In this brief first chapter, we have seen that the God, who is one, and has always been one, plans on reducing everything that still exists into a state of oneness for all of eternity future. At this point, we have begun to establish the importance of the number "one" to God, and in the pages ahead, we will establish why this is so important to the future of the church of the living God, **the God who is One.**

CHAPTER 2

GOD'S ARITHMETIC

ONE PLUS ONE = ONE

*C*hristians are very familiar with the marriage concept: "two shall become one flesh." But most Christians have not discovered that the concept, "two shall become one," is a frequent biblical principle in several other contexts as well.

EZEKIEL 37

Ezekiel's "Valley of Dry Bones" is a popular subject for sermons and Bible studies, but very few Christians know what the second half of Ezekiel 37 is all about. While the first fourteen verses deal with spiritual revival, the last fourteen verses deal with two separate nations becoming united into one nation.

In verse 16 and 17, Ezekiel was told to take two sticks and join them together in one hand and they would become one stick in his hand. The two sticks represented the nation of Judah in the south, and Ephraim (Israel) in the north. Notice the following verses:

*"Then join them **one** to another for yourself into **one** stick, and they will become **one** in your hand." (Ezekiel 37:17)*

*"Say to them, 'Thus says the Lord God, 'Surely I will take the stick of Joseph, which is in the hand of Ephraim, and the tribes of Israel, his companions; and I will join them with it, with the stick of Judah, and make them **one** stick, and they will be **one** in my hand.'"* (Ezekiel 37:19)

*"and I will make them **one** nation in the land, on the mountains of Israel: and **one** king shall be king over them all; **they shall no longer be two nations, nor shall they ever be divided into two kingdoms again."*** (Ezekiel 37:26)

This is an example of divine mathematics. This is what God desires to duplicate many times over in our world. As carnal and earthly human beings, we normally tend to divide, making one into two, fighting to prove that we are right, rather than fighting for unity. **But God, who Himself is One, wants to make two into one, not one into two.**

FROM DIVISION TO DEVASTATION

When Solomon forsook the Lord in his later years, God's punishment was to allow division in the kingdom left to his heirs. The division would leave his son with only the southern part, which was less than half of the whole nation of Israel. As we will reveal, this was the beginning of the end for both Judah in the south and the rest of Israel in the north.

Under David's united Kingdom, every neighboring nation had been conquered. As "One nation" united "under God," Israel was invincible. After forty years as king, first over Judah, and then over all Israel, David and his united armies had subdued all their enemies. When Solomon came to the throne he had no wars to fight and he could focus entirely on building a beautiful house or temple for the Lord, as well as his own beautiful palace.

When Solomon left the scene, his son Rehoboam was given foolish advise by his young advisers. Ten tribes responded by revolting and setting up their own kingdom under Jeroboam, the son of Nebat. Very few people understand the significance of that action. It is always sad when divisions occur, but we seldom realize the extent of the devastation that follows division.

Paul was very aware of the potential devastation of disunity. Repeatedly he begged and exhorted his readers to stay in unity. In Ephesians 4:1-3, Paul declares that in order to walk worthy of the calling given to us, we must "keep the unity of the Spirit in the bond of peace." The word "keep" (*tereo* in the Greek) means, "to guard from loss or injury, by keeping the eyes upon" (Strong's Concordance).

When we don't guard, or keep our eyes upon unity, we always suffer loss or injury. We must pay close attention to the unity we have been given by God or we will become very vulnerable to our enemy, who is always waiting for a weakness to exploit.

So what devastation resulted in both Judah and Israel after they parted company?

First of all, they both had one more enemy than they had before, and one more border to guard. They couldn't focus on staying strong to protect themselves from their mutual enemies, because now they had to worry about each other as well. As soon as the northern tribes revolted, Rehoboam gathered his army to try to force their submission. War was only averted when a prophet warned him not to fight his brothers. We are told in II Chronicles that the division itself was from the Lord, because of the sin of Solomon and the people who so quickly forsook the Lord. Rehoboam heeded the word from God through the prophet and obediently allowed Jeroboam to rule over the northern kingdom.

Before long, however, the northern kingdom, with a mighty army of eight hundred thousand strong, decided to engage Judah in battle. Judah, had only four hundred thousand soldiers. The result was one of the greatest massacres in human history, but as is often the case in God's Kingdom, the smaller power defeated the greater power. The northern kingdom of Israel lost five-eighths of its army, a full half-million or five hundred thousand warriors. It was one of the greatest slaughters of that period of history, which was long before the days of gunpowder and modern weapons of war. As a result, Israel would never again recover its military greatness, and eventually they would be taken into captivity by the Assyrians.

The southern kingdom of Judah, unlike the Northern Kingdom, had several righteous kings along with a number of wicked ones. They prospered under the leadership of the godly kings, but were weakened every time a wicked man or woman would rule over them. But even though they prospered in many ways under good leaders, they never again had that protection of a solid buffer zone, which had been in place when David turned the kingdom over to Solomon. Instead, even the great kings like Asa, Jehoshaphat and Hezekiah had to cry out to God to defend Judah against attacks from very powerful enemies.

Ultimately, the southern kingdom of Judah also fell. Babylon came and hauled away Jerusalem's sacred treasures and most of Judah's people, who became known as Jews. What had once been a virtual empire under God, in the days of David and Solomon, had been drastically weakened by division. The enemies of God's divided people were able to come and take the spoils. This all happened in fulfillment of many warnings, which God, through Moses, had given the people. They had been told that if they forsook the Lord, they would flee before their enemies. What is not common knowledge, however, is the fact that God allowed division to be the means by which they would become so vulnerable.

THE UNITED STATES OF AMERICA

The history of the United States of America could have been very similar to that of the nation of Israel. Even as there was a division between north and south in Israel, there was also a division between north and south in the young nation, which had just a century earlier forged a unity to fight off tyranny and injustice. Because the states united under General George Washington, who called on God for help, and led others to do the same, God allowed them to defeat the greatest military power in the world at that time.

But by the middle of the nineteenth century, an ugly divisive issue was threatening to bring about a major north/south split in this God-ordained republic. The love of money and economic prosperity had perverted the morality of slave owners in the south. Many of these claimed belief in Jesus, the one who came to set captives free, but they still kept slaves in captivity and were willing to divide their nation to protect their right to do so. Americans became more and more embroiled in the controversy until a prophetic apostle, named Abraham Lincoln, came on the scene.

President Lincoln had great foresight into what would happen if he allowed the South to separate from the North. He rose up and declared that the United States of America must remain united or he would lead the charge to go to war to keep them as one nation. The American Civil War or War Between the States was a terrible time for America. Thousands of soldiers died, families suffered incredibly, and much property was destroyed. Many may have thought at the time that it was not worth the suffering and loss.

IMAGINE A NORTH USA AND A SOUTH USA

But can anyone really imagine what might have happened if Abraham Lincoln had not had the courage to make the tough decision when he did. Can we imagine two nations living next to each other, with hostile attitudes toward each other? Would slavery ever have been abolished? Can we picture what the world would be like today, if America had not become a benevolent super-power to protect weaker nations as well as ourselves? Two separate nations would not have had the economic or the military might to be a major influence in Europe or Asia.

Would Germany and Japan have conquered Europe and Asia in World War II? Would they have gone on to subdue both the Northern and Southern halves of America as well as Canada, Mexico and all of Latin America? Or would perhaps Russian and Chinese Communism have conquered the whole world instead? So many possibilities exist, but none of them would be in any way desirable.

As much as the Civil War was a terrible time for those enduring it a century and a half ago, the suffering of those days would pale in comparison to the suffering which future generations would have endured had not Abraham Lincoln drawn a circle in the sand and declared that "one nation under God" would remain "one nation under God." Not one state would be allowed to leave the circle of protection and unity. Abraham Lincoln was one who was faithful to "guard the unity" that God had given the young nation. Today, the whole world is safer and freer than it would have been with the existence of a "North U.S.A." and a "South U.S.A."

ONE + ONE = ONE   WITH JEWS AND GENTILES

There have been and still are many major division in the human race, but one which has been around for several millennia is the division between Jews and Gentiles. There has been much animosity and hostility between these two groups of humanity. Jews have often felt a sense of superiority because of their spiritual inheritance and special place in God's redemptive plan. Gentiles have often felt hatred and jealousy towards them and on many occasions have tried to massacre and completely eliminate "God's Chosen People." The six million Jews who died in Hitler's "Holocaust" is just one example.

But in Ephesians 2:13-18, Paul, speaking to Gentiles in Ephesus, declares:

*"But now in Christ Jesus you who once were far off have been made near by the blood of Christ. For He Himself is our peace, **who has made both one**, and **has broken down the middle***

wall of division between us, having abolished in His flesh the enmity, that is the law of commandments contained in ordinances, so as to create in Himself one new man, from the two, thus making peace, and that He might reconcile them both to God in one body, through the cross, thereby putting to death the enmity. And He came and preached peace to you who were afar off and to those who were near. For through Him we both have access by one Spirit to the Father."

This powerful passage clearly reinforces the basis of God's math. He loves to take one group of people and join them with another group of people and transform two groups into one group. Through the work of Jesus on the cross, the "wall of division" that had divided the two groups has been "broken down." In Ephesians 3:1-6, Paul declares that this is a mystery that God "has revealed by the Spirit to His holy apostles and prophets" (Eph. 3:5), which had been hidden to people before the cross. It is another great example of two becoming one – God's great principle of arithmetic, where one plus one equals one.

ONE + ONE = ONE   IN MARRIAGE

Scripture refers several times to the fact that God puts two people together and that they become one flesh. The first reference is in Genesis 2:24:

"Therefore a man shall leave his father and mother and be joined to his wife, and they shall become one flesh."

Like the two sticks in Ezekiel 37, two are joined to each other and become one. Malachi gives us more insights into the value and importance of two becoming one in marriage.

"But did He not make them one, having a remnant of the Spirit? And why one? He seeks godly offspring. Therefore take heed to your spirit, and let none deal treacherously with the wife of his youth." (Mal. 2:18)

Here we discover that there was a remnant or residue of the Spirit in the unity of marriage that God ordained. Perhaps it relates to the unity that is in God the Father, Son and Holy Spirit. At any rate, Malachi goes on to say that God made husband and wife one for a reason. That reason is that He seeks godly offspring. He made us one physically to have physical offspring. The basic principle is everywhere in nature. The male and female parts of plants and animals must come together in order for reproduction to occur.

But God does not simply desire offspring, **He seeks GODLY offspring!** This, I believe, is a very important revelation that the church of Jesus has never grasped. There is actually a purpose for unity. It is reproduction of something that looks a lot like Him. But for us to produce godly offspring, there must be a coming together of soul and spirit as well as body. And there must be a submission to that same Spirit of God that we have available to us in our marriage relationship.

This truth is critical to understand and apply if we are to work with God for the growth and expansion of the Kingdom. How many couples have looked into each others eyes at the marriage altar and declared in their vows,

> *"We are getting married today so that we can produce godly children for the Lord. We want to be fruitful and multiply and produce children who will have the Spirit of God in them, and who will powerfully subdue the earth and bring it under the Lordship of Jesus Christ."*

There is nothing wrong with romance and rejoicing with the wife (or husband) of our youth, but God has a greater purpose for bringing us together, as He reveals through the prophet, Malachi.

Families are God's idea, not ours, and He had a purpose for them. He made us all for Himself and His own pleasure, even though He clearly enjoys blessing us with many special treasures and pleasures. And if our heart is truly seeking after Him in every area, including "our" family, His heart's desire will be to bless us more than we can imagine.

But most of us think of our children as "our" children. We forget that if we are truly His love slaves, "our" children are really "His" children. A slave has no rights to anything, including his or her children. But our Master is so awesome that He rewards us far more than we deserve, just to show His love. And when "our" children are "His" children, they have the King for their father. And we know that He has the resources to give them the best of everything and meet their every need.

IMPORTANT APPLICATIONS

God first introduced the mathematical principle that One + One = One, way back in Genesis, the first book of the Old Testament. He finally revealed the purpose for it in Malachi, the last book of the Old Testament. He repeated it again in I Corinthians 6:16, and then added, "But he who is joined to the Lord is one spirit with Him." This is one more instance where one + one = one. When we are joined to the Lord as a man is to a wife, we become one spirit with Him. So let's now begin to make some applications of that principle.

FAMILY LIFE

First of all, if our goal in marriage is to raise godly offspring, than our home life should reflect that. We should focus more on teaching and training our children in the ways of the Kingdom. Priorities should shift from earning a living and teaching our children to earn a living to developing the character and passion of Jesus in ourselves and in our seed.

We should also carefully guard the unity in our marriage, especially in the soul and spirit realm. It is much more difficult for children to become godly when there is major disunity in the marriage. Both husbands and wives should guard against the treacherous temptations to be unfaithful or to be independent of each other.

Children may survive spiritually when there is a lack of unity, but they will very likely have serious character issues to deal with.

Timothy may have been such an example. He had a godly mother and grandmother, but His father was a Greek and probably not a believer (Acts 16:1). He was discipled and raised up into apostolic ministry, but Paul had to remind him several times not to neglect his gifts, but to stir them up. He appeared to have some fear of man, because Paul had to remind him that God had not given him "a spirit of fear, but of power, and of love and of a sound mind." (II Tim. 1:6,7). This fear of man may have resulted from a lack of fatherly input. Courage traditionally has been a masculine strength, which Timothy's mother, Eunice, and his grandmother, Lois, may not have adequately been able to impart to him.

MINISTRY MULTIPLICATION AND REPRODUCTION

The second principle is that if we want to reproduce in our ministries and raise up spiritual seed and expand the Kingdom of God, we must apply the principle of two becoming one. We must believe that God can take people who are as opposite from each other as a man and a woman are in their personalities and bring them into a true spiritual unity.

This principle can apply in a small local ministry, or it can apply to major denominations and movements. Although it may seem inconceivable that two different branches of Christianity could become one in God's hand, if we truly have God's passionate heart on the matter and are willing to be instruments in His hands to bring peace and unity, we will discover that God has many ways of breaking down "middle walls of division."

It is true that God can use us in different regiments, or army divisions, but He definitely wants to coordinate our military activities. To do so, we need to surrender our authority and sovereignty to Him. When we do that, we may find ourselves working side by side with those who previously had been hostile to us and us to them. He can miraculously break down the walls and give us working relationships that will powerfully multiply our effectiveness and result in true spiritual reproduction. Remember that without opposites coming together in some level of intimacy, there is no reproduction in nature. And don't forget that one shall chase a thousand, but two shall put ten thousand to flight (Deut. 32:30).

LEGOS

I was recently given an illustration by the Lord about building the house of the Lord. In a small home group I suggested that if someone had dumped out a big box of Legos in the middle of the room, we would have two options as to what to do with them. The first option would be to divide up the Legos so that each person would get his or her share. Then we could try to build something bigger and better than anyone else in the room. The second options was that we could decide to work together and build something extremely large and splendid.

Working together is not as easy, because you don't always get your way and you have to listen to and respect the others' opinions. But we will never be able to build anything very glorious if we insist on taking our small supply of Legos off by ourselves and trying to do our own thing. David, who had a heart for the house of God like no one else, told the people, **"The house that is to be built must be exceedingly magnificent, famous and glorious throughout all countries"** (I Chronicles 22:5).

We must learn to put our gifts together into one team. We must surrender our blocks to the team who can design something far more beautiful than we can imagine. What a glorious house we could build for the Lord if we all worked together to build the house that He has designed and revealed to His apostles and prophets.

After the meeting, the young teenage daughter of our host came to me and said, "Sometimes people do something else when they are building with their Legos. They sometimes knock down what the other person is building to make their own look better." How truly perceptive of a young lady who really loves the Lord.

TAKE HEED HOW YOU BUILD

Another related Scripture is found in I Corinthians 3:10. Paul warns us to be careful how we build on the foundation that he had laid, the foundation being Jesus Christ, Himself. He reminds us that whatever we build will be tried by fire. We are to build the house with that which has value, like gold, silver and precious stones, not that which is easy to use like wood, hay and stubble.

It is extremely interesting and relevant, in my opinion, that this discussion comes immediately after he rebukes them and says that they are still "carnal" because they have divisions among them and identify themselves with different leaders. He goes on to say that he had planted, and Apollos had watered, but it was God who had given the increase. Then he declares:

"Now, he who plants and he who waters are __one__." (I Corinthians 3:8)

Here is yet another case of **one + one = one**. But the point here is that they were not going to be able to build with quality if they divided up into "Paulites and Apollosites." The house that they would build would not be "exceedingly magnificent, famous and glorious throughout all countries," because they were rejecting some of the gold and silver and precious stones that were in another camp.

Paul goes on to remind them:

"You (plural) are the temple of God and the Spirit of God dwells in you." (I Corinthians 3:16)

We are the building blocks, or stones, in the temple of God. We are to build with the gold of God's nature, character and glory. We are to build ourselves up in our most holy faith, praying in the Holy Spirit (Jude 20), and we are to build or edify one another according to I Corinthians 14 and other passages.

THE FLOWER VISION

Several years ago, while at a camp near San Diego, California, God gave me a brief but very significant vision. I saw a very beautiful flower. The petals were large and colorful. They were very attractive, but I found my eyes focusing not on the beautiful petals, but on the center or heart of the flower, which did not have the same natural appeal as the petals.

But I knew God was saying, "I'm not looking at the outward appearance. I'm looking at the heart." I knew also that at the heart of the flower was everything of real value. I felt that the flower represented churches, ministries, movements or denominations and the petals represented all the things that we do to attract people, like the pretty petals attract the insects. It might include our beautiful building, great worship music, excellent children's ministries, youth and singles ministries, and many other good things. But God makes a "beeline" to the heart of the flower. That's where the bee gets the nectar to make honey, and that's where it picks up the pollen for transfer to other flowers.

What God wants to know is not how beautiful our petals are, but how sweet is our heart. And how open are we to being invaded by those who bring pollen from other flowers. I perceived that many churches, denominations, movements, ministries, etc., are not very willing to receive input from folks from other churches, denominations, movements or ministries.

What God seemed to be strongly saying to His church is this: **"If you are not willing to be cross-pollinated, through the**

apostles, prophets and teachers that I am sending from place to place throughout my Kingdom, your ministry will eventually shrivel up and die without reproducing yourself in the next generation." A flower that is not cross-pollinated cannot produce fruit. No matter how beautiful its petals, they will fade and die and there will be no future for that flower.

Even so, many churches, denominations, movements and ministries are seeing their life energy ebbing away. And while God moves powerfully on other groups, they close up their petals and refuse to allow anything to contaminate their purity. **The result is a barren womb and a fading glory.** It is such a tragedy, because it is so unnecessary.

Those however, who are allowing God to invade their cloistered halls with folk from other streams and movements are beginning to realize the vastness of God's Kingdom revelation. They are becoming greatly enriched and empowered. Reproduction is taking place at an ever-increasing rate, and blessings flow from Heaven to earth.

Men like Dr. C. Peter Wagner are to be highly commended for their efforts in bringing together many different streams of Christianity. They have begun to listen to each other to get a bigger picture of what God is saying to His church in these tremendously eventful days. Today, leaders from many different flavors of His church are speaking together at major conferences held throughout North America and the world. The results are powerful. We have personally witnessed that every recent conference and gathering of Christians which we have attended has been visited by God in a steadily increasing glory. Others have related to us that they are having similar experiences. The power of unity is being rediscovered and unleashed on the earth. Cross-pollination is working! Reproduction is accelerating!

HE THAT HAS EARS

In Revelation 2 and 3, we are given seven letters to seven churches. At the end of each letter, we are told, *"He that has ears to hear, let him hear what the Spirit says to the churches."* I noticed that the word was in the plural. He did not say, "Hear what the Spirit says to the church," or "Hear what the Spirit says to your church." We are to listen to what the Spirit of God has to say to all the churches. This is cross-pollination! When Paul wrote a letter to the Colossians, he advised them to also read his letter to the Laodiceans, and to have the Laodiceans read the letter that he had written to them (Colossians 4:16).

God is speaking different threads of truth to different groups and movements today. Only when we weave them together will we see the beautiful tapestry of truth that He is imparting to His church today. The only way that THE CHURCH will be whole and healthy is if THE CHURCHES tear down the walls that divide them and truly learn to listen to each other. That doesn't mean that we accept false teachings, but we are guided by humility and love of Jesus, who is the Truth.

I am very convinced that doctrinal differences are slowly but surely melting away with the increasing awareness of the presence of the Lord in our midst. His presence humbles us and allows us to listen to others. So many of our disagreements are because we have seen only one side of the issue and others are seeing the issue from a different perspective. The illuminating light of the glory of the manifest presence of Jesus shows us the bigger picture from a higher perspective that will help us to understand why we see things differently. Love will overpower our remaining intellectual differences, because we will feel God's love for His children and we will lose our critical or contentious spirit towards our brothers and sisters.

ONE + ONE = ONE   IN FORMATION OF LIFE

When procreation occurs, the principle of God's math is vividly illustrated. One cannot reproduce one. It takes two entities becoming one to reproduce. There may be millions of sperm seeking to unite with the egg, but all of them will die except the one that wins the race and joins itself to that one egg. Those who remain independent will not survive as living organisms. Only the one that dies to its independence and becomes virtually lost in the much larger egg will live. Even so the egg, if it does not allow penetration by the tiny sperm, will not survive very long, but will also die.

This so clearly illustrates the ways of God's Kingdom. He who saves his life will lose it, but he who loses his life will save it. We must learn to humble ourselves and work with different or even opposite personalities before we can reproduce something special for God. This can be a real death experience. We would much rather separate to preserve our independence, but God wants humility which makes way for unity, so we can produce godly offspring for Him.

OTHER   APPLICATIONS

There are many polarizations in the world and in the Church of Jesus Christ. In the world we have conservatives and liberals, Republicans and Democrats, labor and management, environmentalists and industrialists, etc.

But we have even worse polarizations in the church. We have Catholics versus Protestants. We have Evangelicals versus Pentecostals. We have "enlightenment" liberals versus fundamentalists. We have "exclusivists versus inclusivists", Calvinists versus Armenians, Post-Tribulation Rapturists and Pre-Tribulation Rapturists. We also have numerous brands of Baptists, Pentecostals, Mennonites, Episcopalians, Presbyterians, Lutherans, Methodists, Brethren, etc.

Is God pleased that we have so thoroughly chopped up His own body into thousands of separate pieces? Did He mean what He said when He declared that there is only ONE body? Is there anything that anyone can do to reverse the process of splits and division?

1. The first thing we must do is agree with God that there is only ONE body of Jesus and share His heart that His body be healed and restored to the unity it originally possessed. This will result in prayer and intercession for the healing of His body.

2. The next thing we must do is to examine our words and actions and the motives for them. Are we more interested in proving ourselves right, or are we more interested in bringing unity in Christian relationships? We must pursue humility and censor pride.

3. The third thing we can do is to show practical demonstrations of our desire for unity. We can pursue relationships with those who wear a different ecclesiastical label to get to know them and find out where they are coming from. We can do like many churches are doing in these days, and make financial or other contributions to other churches and ministries that need help. It's amazing how powerful a gift can be as a tool to break down walls that the enemy has built.

4. The fourth thing we can do is gather leaders together to pray and worship and work together for the King. Let musicians from the different ministries get together to prepare for a worship night. Let them pray together and ask God for harmony as they lead people into the presence of God. Musicians are not so prone to worry about the differences in doctrines and they may be able to lead people into unity better than ecclesiastical

leaders, because they will focus on worship, putting people's eyes on the Lord instead of on their doctrinal differences.

5. The fifth, and arguably, the most powerful, way to bring unity is using God's miracle power to touch the lives of others. At almost any given time, people whose beliefs are somewhat opposed to ours are in need of a miracle. They might be sick or have a sick child. They may have a financial emergency, or some other need. If we show compassion and pray for them and with them for a miracle and God reveals His love to them by supplying a miracle for them, we will have a friend for life. The person who receives the miracle is going to love God more and also love the one who God used to bring their miracle. The result is two becoming one.

As we will see in the next few chapters, there are few things more important to God than bringing the body of Jesus into unity. There are so many situations where God wants to take two and make them one. Let's move on now to the relationship of unity to what we call "The Harvest."

CHAPTER 3

GOD'S FAVORITE NUMBER AND THE HARVEST

*O*ne of the most misused or misunderstood biblical terms is, "The Harvest." When I discovered what I am about to share, it almost blew me away. It was totally consistent with what God had been teaching me about His passion for unity, but it was not what I had been taught as I grew up in various Christian churches and movements.

THE GATHERING TOGETHER

The idea of gathering things or people together is an often repeated theme throughout Scripture. Over and over in the Old Testament prophetic books, God promises to gather together that which He had scattered because of idolatry. But I was still not aware of how often this phrase is used until God begin to share this revelation with me. The first Scripture that came alive was found both in Luke 13:34, 35 and Matthew 23:37, 38. Matthew's version declares:

*"O Jerusalem, Jerusalem, the one who kills the prophets and stones those who are sent to her! **How often I wanted to gather your children together**, as a hen gathers her chicks under her*

wings, but you were not willing! See! Your house is left to you desolate."

For some reason, in the past when I read this verse, my mind would focus on the word picture of the hen covering her chicks. That spoke of protection, which was a result of the first part, but I missed the focus of Jesus on the gathering together. If we leave out the word picture, used to illustrate the point, Jesus is saying, "How often I would have gathered your children together, but you were not willing."

The result of Jerusalem's leaders not allowing Jesus to gather His own people together was that their house would become desolate. As we have seen, God's ultimate plan is that everything be gathered together in one – into Jesus. What is not gathered together in Jesus will become desolate or destroyed, even as Jerusalem was in 70 A.D, by the Romans, under a general named Titus.

The reason the leaders of Jerusalem would not allow Jesus the freedom of gathering His children together was that **they all wanted to keep control of their piece of the ecclesiastical pie**. If people were gathered together under the leadership of Jesus, they would lose their positions and power. There were many different sects, each with their own leaders, almost like we have today in Christendom.

Imagine what might have happened if they had recognized the One who wanted to unite the people and make them one? What if the Pharisees and Sadducees and all other sects would have agreed to recognize Jesus as the Messiah and recommend that the people follow Him? The common people would have gladly accepted Him and history would have read quite differently. Of course, we know that Jesus had to die for our redemption, but could God not have worked it out a different way? Perhaps the Romans would have crucified Him out of fear of His influence, without the support of the Sanhedrin.

But of course that didn't happen, because He was not received by His own. He was not given the favor of Jerusalem's leaders and instead of uniting the people in Himself, His own sheep were further scattered when the shepherd was smitten. Later however, His people were gathered together into the body of Jesus in the early church. Luke comments frequently in the book of Acts about the disciples being together and having all things in common (Acts 2:44).

UNDERSTANDING THE HARVEST

Read carefully the following passage:

*"And when He saw the multitudes, He was moved with compassion for them, because **they were weary and scattered**, like sheep having no shepherd." (Matthew 9:36)*

Notice that Jesus' compassion was based on the fact that He saw the people as those who were weary and scattered as sheep having no shepherd. **The opposite of "to gather" is "to scatter."** In Matthew 23:37, Jesus wanted to **gather** his children together. In Matthew 9:36, He was moved with compassion because **they were scattered, or not gathered**. As was the case in the other passage, Jesus was seeing with spiritual eyes, rather than natural eyes. What He saw caused Him to be deeply moved. He saw His people as weary or fainting sheep. They were weary and fainting because they were not being nourished by their true shepherd. Instead they were being completely controlled and manipulated by hirelings who wanted their wool and mutton without having to feed them the pure food from Heaven.

Furthermore, as we have already noted, they were **scattered**. They did not have the benefits of being together in one flock with one Shepherd. They had no great sense of security and protection. There was no overwhelming sense of Shalom – peace and prosperity and general well being. Instead little groups of sheep would compete with other little groups for the same pastures and quiet streams. The grass would get trampled before it could get eaten and the streams would be muddied as they fought for position in the shallow waters. (See Ezekiel 34.)

The sheep were never totally sure they were in the best possible flock. Perhaps the other flocks were getting the greener pastures. Their hireling shepherds seemed to be always more concerned with their own comfort and security than with that of the sheep. The howling of the wolves could be heard from time to time and many times it was noted that one or more of their company had disappeared, quite possibly the victims of ravenous wolves or lions or bears.

But what proves to be the most surprising statement when viewed in this context comes in the following verse:

*"Then He said to His disciples, '**The harvest** truly is plentiful, but the laborers are few. Therefore pray the Lord of **the harvest** to send out laborers into His harvest." (Matthew 9:37, 38)*

Jesus responds to His feelings of compassion for His weary and scattered sheep by telling His disciples that the harvest truly is plentiful, but the laborers are few. He then instructs them to pray to the Lord of the Harvest that He would send forth laborers into His harvest.

Jesus is clearly not talking here about converting the Heathen to faith in God. His concern here is the fact that His own sheep are scattered because He has not been presented to them as their Shepherd by the leaders of the Jews.

Suddenly, I realized that when a farmer brings in the harvest, he is not converting the weeds or tares into wheat. Rather he is gathering together into one location all the pure grain that He has been growing for a number of weeks or months. **Harvest is not so much about conversion, it is about gathering.** Let me quickly add that much of the coming harvest will include many that are yet to be converted, but **the actual harvest is the gathering together of those who are His.**

The farmer cannot accomplish much with the grain while it is blowing in the wind on a thin stalk. But when the grain is gathered into his barns, he can sell it or grind it into flower and make bread with it. He can also take some of it and sow it in the ground to bring forth a future harvest. Even so, God cannot do much with us when we are totally independent of one another, waving our flag of individualism in the wind. But when we gather into a unity of heart and purpose, He can blend us together and prepare us to be food for the hungry.

As most of us are well aware, the books of the Bible were not written in chapters. Chapter numbers and verses were added later to give us "addresses" to identify the location of the statements made in Scripture. Therefore, when we come to the end of one chapter we can just keep reading into the next chapter as if there was no break.

Proceeding then to Matthew 10, we go on to read that Jesus called His twelve disciples together and instructed them to go and proclaim the Kingdom of God and to demonstrate it by doing miracles of love and kindness among the people. Notice that this was recorded by Matthew immediately after Jesus' discussion about the harvest and the need for workers in the harvest fields. In other words, it certainly appears that Jesus is responding to the need for workers in the harvest field by sending His own disciples into that same harvest field.

Now notice the instructions of Jesus in verses five and six, after the twelve are named in verses two through four:

"These twelve Jesus sent out and commanded them, saying: 'Do not go into the way of the Gentiles, and do not enter a city of the Samaritans. But go rather to the lost sheep of the house of Israel. And as you go, preach, saying, 'The kingdom

of heaven is at hand.' Heal the sick, cleanse the lepers, raise the
dead, cast out demons. Freely you have received, freely give.'"
(Matthew 10:5,6)

He was sending His harvesters not to the totally lost Gentiles or
even to the half-Jewish Samaritans, but only to the "lost" sheep of
the house of Israel. That word, "lost," is the Greek word *apollumi*
which primarily means destroyed or marred. The implication is
that the sheep have been badly hurt or wounded. The disciples
were to first preach that the Kingdom of Heaven was at hand and
then heal the sick, cleanse the lepers, raise the dead and cast out
devils. These miracles would prove the fact that the Kingdom of
Heaven had arrived on earth. It was literally "at hand."

So then, how does preaching the arrival of the Kingdom of
Heaven relate to the gathering of the harvest? It really is quite simple.
It has to do with the fact that when their King or Messiah would
arrive, they would become united into one free nation under their
King, the Son of David. But for us to really understand this we
must look at something about a kingdom that those of us who live
in a republic or democracy may not be aware of.

First of all, in a true kingdom there is no opposition party. There
are no liberals and conservatives. There are no Republicans and
Democrats. In a kingdom there is no room for a variety of
conflicting opinions or groups. There is simply a king who has all
authority and there are his subjects who accept his authority. If the
king is a wise, strong and benevolent leader, the people are greatly
blessed and live in peace and safety.

Secondly, in a kingdom people tend to highly revere, honor or
even worship their king. He is the one to whom they look for
protection when they are attacked by their enemies. They also
look to him for justice when falsely accused, etc. He is the most
powerful person they know and they gladly bow down to him in
reverence and honor. The result is a strong sense of unity, since the
king has gathered them together under one head.

When you factor in the fact that Jesus is talking about a Heavenly King, you take the above phenomena to a much higher level. Now we are talking about a King who brings the power of Heaven to earth. He is a King who can overturn every injustice and reveal His awesome power when it is needed. That is why Jesus had the disciples do so many miracles. He was showing His power over all the toughest challenges that the Jews faced every day.

The miracles the disciples performed showed his power over incurable sicknesses and diseases like leprosy. They also showed His power over death itself and over the demonic realm. He truly was revealing that He was the King and that His power proved who He was. At the same time He was revealing that He even had the power to transfer His authority and power to His followers.

But the most important point we want to make here is that when you have a king in charge you have a unity which you don't have in any other form of government. The king gathers his subjects into his kingdom or "king's domain." They are **gathered together** to honor him, to be protected by him and to unite to defend their "king's domain" from all attackers.

Without being united under one king over all the land, the people will be divided under many different lords and rulers, as it was in Europe in Medieval times. It was in a parallel manner divided up in Israel in Jesus' day in the spiritual realm under the different religious groups. But when a king comes to possess his rightful throne, he subdues all the other leaders and the nation is united with only one all-powerful sovereign.

So what we are saying is that Jesus sent His disciples with His power and authority to prove His Kingship and to gather His sheep into one sheepfold, where they would be united and sheltered and nourished by the Great Shepherd. His disciples were His harvesters and gathering the harvest was literally the act of bringing His own people together into unity.

When I first saw this scenario, I realized that Jesus' passion for unity, which He clearly expressed in His John 17 prayer, was even greater than I had previously thought. **Whenever He looked upon the people with compassion or wept over the city of Jerusalem, it was because of their lack of unity under their rightful King.** They had a prophetic and legal right to have the Son of David as their King. Jesus had come to fulfill the prophecies of the Old Testament, but the jealous leaders would not allow Him to take His rightful throne and gather His children together in unity as a hen would gather her chicks under her wings.

Let's take another look at the concept of "The Harvest" and clarify our thoughts. Harvest primarily is a time to gather good wheat together into the Master's barns. Conversion of the lost is not converting tares into wheat, but actually manifesting what was already known by God to be His true wheat. Tares looked like wheat, but were not the real thing. The real tares will never become wheat, but will be harvested (gathered) separately and burned.

One important aspect of the time of Harvest is "the joy of the Harvest." Notice what Isaiah declares:

"You have multiplied the nation and increased its joy; They rejoice before You according **to the joy of harvest,** *as men rejoice when they divide the spoil." (Isaiah 9:3)*

Harvest is a time of celebration. Hard work and sacrifice have finally produced the desired results, and the family rejoices over the fact that there will be provision for another winter. This aspect of the harvest certainly applies to souls getting saved, because we know that the angels in Heaven rejoice over one sinner that repents.

Certainly, getting people saved brings them into the fold of Heaven and as such, they have been harvested into the grain bin of the Kingdom. But on the deeper level, if they are positioned in a system of man that separates them from the rest of the body of

Christ, and not taught to have a personal as well as a corporate intimacy with their King, I believe that Jesus would again see them as sheep scattered with no shepherd even though they know intellectually who their Shepherd is.

Although this new concept is still not extremely well-defined in my own mind, it seems clear that bringing in the harvest has just as much to do with bringing the converts and older saints into unity as it has to do with evangelizing the heathen. Bringing in the harvest is bringing people together that have a united and consuming passion to worship and honor and serve their King.

THE HARVEST AND THE SAMARITAN WOMAN

Jesus also referred to the harvest in John 4. This is the passage which most strongly implies that the harvest is converting the lost, but we want to show that this was not the only aspect of the harvest that Jesus was referring to.

Jesus told his disciples not to say that the harvest was yet months away. Rather, He declared that the fields were already white and ready for harvest. This was in the context of His ministry to the "woman at the well" and the resulting conversion of much of the city of Samaria. He was expanding His ministry from Jerusalem and Judea to Samaria and would later send His apostles to "the uttermost parts of the world."

In this passage, the harvest process clearly includes making believers of the Samaritans. But Jesus was not just getting them to believe in Him, He was also breaking down the walls that separated them from the Jews. Jesus had just been teaching the Samaritan woman about true worship. He had told her that salvation was of the Jews, but in the future it would not be on which mountain they worshipped, but from what kind of a heart they worshipped. Thus, it made no difference if you were a Jew or a Samaritan.

Jesus was clearly taking down the "middle wall of division" between the Jews and the Samaritans, revealing again that **one + one = one** in still one more scenario. The Samaritans were a mixed race and thus were not considered pure Israelites or Jews. Thus they were rejected by the self-righteous Jews and all their religious leaders.

But Jesus was proving He was the Messiah through the gift of knowledge. His vision was of a much bigger harvest. He wanted all to believe in Him and worship Him as the King, both of the Jews and of the Samaritans, and ultimately, also of the Gentiles. Getting them to believe in Him was the first step in the gathering of the harvest.

Even though the Samaritans belonged to Him by legal right, they still needed their hearts converted before they could become His true subjects in His Kingdom. Remember that the predominant teaching of Jesus was the Kingdom of Heaven. If, as we have already shown, unity was a given essential ingredient of any kingdom, then unity was a concept inseparable from His favorite theme.

When the Samaritans began to believe in Jesus, it was harvest time in Samaria. It was definitely a time of bringing salvation and unity. It was not the conversion of tares into wheat, but it was the means by which the Jews and Samaritans, who were already His people, were gathered together into one Kingdom, the Kingdom of Heaven.

It is very interesting that before Peter ministered to Cornelius, the first Gentile convert, in Acts 10, we read in Acts 8 that Philip went down to Samaria and had a tremendous revival there with powerful miracles and conversions taking place. This was readily accepted by Peter and John, who came along to pray for the converts to be filled with the Holy Spirit. Later, however, both Peter and all the apostles would have a bit of a problem accepting the fact that God wanted to convert the Gentiles as well as the Jews and Samaritans.

I think the point is clear. Jesus began by gathering those who should be the closest to Him, the Jews. Then he reached out to those considered "half-brothers," the Samaritans, and finally He reached out to the uttermost parts of the earth. He gathered, converted and gathered, converted and gathered. It was all a part of the harvest process of bringing everyone together in Himself.

THE FINAL HARVEST

The other New Testament references to the harvest have to do with the final harvest. That will be when the tares are gathered together to be burned and the wheat will be gathered into the barns (Matthew 13:30). The angels will be the reapers for the final harvest, but we, as representatives of the Lord and members of His one body, are called to be the reapers for the harvest today. Of course, God's angels will be working with us every step of the way, doing in the invisible realm what we cannot accomplish in the visible.

PRACTICAL APPLICATION OF THE HARVEST CONCEPT

If the harvest means gathering the good fruit together, then **when we work at bringing the body of Christ into unity, we are helping to gather the harvest.** If we see the church through Jesus' eyes, we will see that His sheep are once again scattered and hurting like He saw them about two thousand years ago. We can still bring His sheep together by revealing His power and glory and focusing them on their King, rather than on their divisive issues and leaders.

We can ask for His vision, so that we can see a whitened harvest field – those who He already knows are His. We can also discern between the Pharisees (who will never receive Him, even though they know He has supernatural power), and those who simply have not yet discovered who their King really is. Then we can show supernatural signs to those who have open hearts, while not wasting our time on those who have evil and adulterous hearts. (For more information on this subject read, *Signs and Wonders – To Seek or Not to Seek* by Ben Peters) We will be bringing those who believe into the fold together with those who have already been in the fold.

We will not be focusing the converts on divisive doctrines to separate them from other Christians, but we will be focusing them on the greatness of their King and on bringing them into His presence in worship and adoration. This will bring joy to the King and He will share the joys of the harvest with us.

I recently read the book entitled, *The Heavenly Man*, the story of Brother Yun, a Chinese House Church leader, who suffered incredibly for the gospel. The house churches were growing and prospering in spite of much persecution and an extreme shortage of Bibles. Finally, Bibles began to come into the country. That was a great blessing, but eventually denominational literature began to accompany some of the Bibles.

Soon many of the House Church leaders were not getting along with each other, as they had taken different stands on controversial doctrines imported from the West. Divisions hindered the growth of the church until Brother Yun and others brought the leaders together and restored a spirit of cooperation. Bringing the church leaders and their followers together was a major part of bringing in the harvest in China.

CHAPTER 4

THE SECRET KEY TO UNITY

*I*n this chapter we want to reemphasize how important it is to Jesus that we find more ways to move into unity, but we especially want to reveal the key to unity which Jesus gave us in His great prayer in John 17. We will share how God is using this key in powerful ways today and bringing about a level of unity that the church of Jesus has not experienced since the early church. This will be a very exciting chapter for you if you love the Kingdom of God.

Because I love numbers and statistics, I often count things that others would not even think about. When I studied the prayer of Jesus in John 17, I decided to count how many different requests Jesus made of His Father. The setting of this prayer was the "Last Supper," just before Gethsemane and Calvary. It was a prayer that was in a time of extreme spiritual and emotional stress for Jesus. He certainly would not have wasted breath on anything that was not extremely important to Him in that prayer.

I listed seventeen requests and then put them into categories. I discovered that most of the things He prayed for were requested just one time. Three things were asked for twice: 1. That His Father would glorify Him. 2. That His Father would keep His disciples. 3. That they would be sanctified by His truth.

But there was one request that Jesus repeated five times. He prayed in various ways that they would all be made "one." But Jesus did not just pray that they would be made "one." He gave reasons why they should be made one (so the world would believe in Him), and He gave the secret of HOW they could become one. That is what we want to look at in this chapter.

The verse that reveals the key to unity is John 17:22:

"And the glory which You gave Me I have given them that they may be one just as we are one."

This verse clearly declares that **God's glory causes us to be one. The key to unity is the glory of God.** I had read this verse many times before I saw this truth. The wonderful thing about the way God progressively reveals truth to us is that His timing is perfect. A few years or even months ago, this revelation would not have seemed nearly as significant.

What did Jesus mean when He said He had given us the glory that His Father gave Him? And how in the world does that make us one?

UNDERSTANDING THE GLORY

The word glory includes several overlapping meanings. One of these is "honor," such as giving or taking the glory or credit for something. Another meaning is "brightness or radiance, which includes the concept of beauty." A third connotation is "greatness," a combination of wealth, fame and power. All of these meanings can be applied to the verse quoted above.

HONOR

Jesus has given us the honor that His Father gave to Him. We are honored to be His children and accepted in His family. Having a sense of family should promote unity. In many practical ways we also feel honored when He blesses us with special blessings and answers to prayer. When we get something that we know we don't deserve, we feel humbled and grateful to God. It fills us with love for God and others, helping us to feel unity with others who also have the same strong love.

LIGHT

The aspect of glory meaning radiance, beauty or brightness can also contribute to unity, because light implies illumination and revelation. This helps us not only to see truth but to see Jesus Himself in His radiant beauty. Whenever our focus is on Jesus, we have unity with others who have the same focus.

GREATNESS

The connotation of glory that implies greatness (wealth, fame and power) can contribute to unity as well. When God's glory is on the church like it was on Solomon, there is an excitement in the Kingdom. There is a rejoicing in the greatness of our leader and His domain. Again, the focus is on how awesome the King is. Jesus has given His greatness to His church, promising that we would do even greater works than He did, but we know that we only have these greater works through His name and authority.

On the other hand, when we lack the miraculous works in the church, there is less excitement and less focus on Jesus and His greatness. Instead we focus on trying to be good, which puts the focus on ourselves. Then we begin to compare ourselves with others, trying to make ourselves look at least as good, or a wee bit better than others. This is the basis of division. Focusing on our King is the basis of our unity.

GLORY – A WORKING DEFINITION

Taking in and putting together what we have just looked at, let us take the liberty to redefine glory with a practical and useful working definition.

My simplified working definition of God's glory is as follows:

Glory: The atmosphere of Heaven that emanates from the presence of God.

All of the above meanings of glory describe that which God possesses and exudes. Heaven is filled with the atmosphere that emanates from His presence. Therefore, we can say that being in His presence allows us to be touched by His glory. And we could also say that as the Father gave His presence to His Son, so also, the Son passed on that same Presence to us.

The Presence of God, I believe, comes in the person of the Holy Spirit. With the same Holy Spirit that God gave to Jesus, we were told that we would do the same works as He did. The Holy Spirit is God, and when He manifests His presence through His fruit and gifts, He is manifesting God's glory. In Ephesians 4:3 we are exhorted to keep or guard the "unity of the Spirit." **Unity is a product of the presence of the Holy Spirit through His fruit and gifts.**

Now please stay with me here! We have made some interesting logical connections and conclusions.

1. **God's glory (His honor, light and greatness) flows out from His presence.**

2. **His presence comes to us in the form of the Holy Spirit.**

3. **The Holy Spirit brings unity through His gifts and fruit.**

Therefore when Jesus said, "I have given them my glory, that they may be one," He could have meant that He was giving them the Holy Spirit and His fruit and gifts so that they would be one.

Now the obvious question is this: How does the Holy Spirit bring unity? Answering this question will begin to put it all together and give us a vision of where God is taking the church in these days.

To answer this question, let's look at the early church, the greatest example of unity in the body of Christ. But let's begin, not in the book of Acts, but in the last chapters of the gospel of John.

THE EARLY CHURCH, THE HOLY SPIRIT AND UNITY

In John 20:22, Jesus breathed on His disciples and said, "Receive the Holy Spirit." This scene took place on Resurrection Day and Jesus was breathing the Spirit of Life into His disciples. This was the first time that Resurrection Life was being breathed into mortal man. When God made Adam He breathed His life into him and man became a living soul. After Adam's fall, man had never experienced this being breathing upon, and the spirit of death had become a reality in man's life.

But now there was something more powerful than death, which was being breathed upon a few Jewish men. It was the Spirit of Life in the person of the Holy Spirit. Now the same Spirit that gave Jesus resurrection life after the cross was being breathed into His disciples.

The fact that the Holy Spirit was now in them as the Spirit of Life would certainly help them to be united. In addition, because of their desertion of Jesus during the crucifixion, they had become painfully aware of the fact that they were all failures at being disciples. This most certainly humbled them greatly, which made them less contentious and more united. This humbling process also must have allowed the Holy Spirit to more completely fill their spiritual lungs with His presence and glory.

The proof of this lies in the fact that when the story continues in the book of Acts, we find the disciples in the state of unity that Jesus had prayed for in John 17. After watching His ascension, they had obediently gone to the upper room to tarry for the coming of the Holy Spirit in His fullness of power. Luke records in Acts 1:14 that the one hundred and twenty folk in the upper room were in one accord. Acts 2:1 declares:

*"Now when the Day of Pentecost had fully come, they were **all with one accord in one place.**"*

These first two of the five references to being in "one accord" occurred before the Holy Spirit was poured out in power in Acts 2:4. Thus the Spirit of Life in the disciples had brought about a transformation of their nature, which had been prone to pride and division. But after the Holy Spirit was poured out in His "dunamis" power, we find many more expressions of unity in the next few chapters.

Not only are there three more uses of the phrase, "one accord," but Luke also reveals to us that the unity was extremely incredible and highly unusual. Note the following passage:

*"Now the multitude of those who believed were of **one heart and one soul**; neither did anyone say that any of the things he possessed was his own, but they had all things in common. And with great power the apostles gave witness to the resurrection of the Lord Jesus. And great grace was upon them all. Nor was there anyone among them who lacked; for all who were possessors of lands or houses sold them, and brought the things that were sold, and laid them at the apostles' feet; and they distributed to each as anyone had need."* *(Acts 4:32-35)*

This scenario describes an extremely high level of unity. The church was not only a large group of people who were getting along with each other, but a large group of people who were making radical sacrifices and showing incredible love for each other. It was not in any way a passive unity, but an extremely proactive unity. This is the kind of unity that we are seeking. It's the kind of unity which will bring about the powerful revival that will be used to gather God's harvest into His heavenly granaries.

UNITY REINFORCED BY HOLY SPIRIT POWER

If the manifestations of the Holy Spirit's power are basically synonymous with God's glory, then we can see how Jesus gave His glory to His disciples. And the amazing stories that Luke records in the book of Acts reveal that these manifestations were incredibly frequent events in the early Jerusalem church. These events included frequent angelic appearances, miraculous healings and deliverances from both human enemies and demonic powers. They also included visions and dreams, prophetic revelations and divine judgment, such as Ananias and Sapphira experienced.

Those early Acts days were filled with manifestations of God's glory, and truly Jesus had given them the same glory as the Father had given Him. The result was that unity was reinforced and strengthened.

Let's take a closer look at how this works. When our Christianity amounts to little more than theology and trying to obey the commandments of Scripture, we lack the vivid expressions of God's glory that come when supernatural manifestations are taking place. I believe that the greater the manifestations of the Holy Spirit, the greater the unity. That unity can escape if not guarded, but without the blessing of God's manifested glory, there will be even less unity.

The defining difference is this: When we see an expression of God's glory in a supernatural event, we are made more aware of God's power and love. We focus more on our King and His majesty and greatness and we focus less on ourselves and our neighbors and the competition among us. When we all focus on Jesus as King and we all have a passion for Him, we have a unity of the Holy Spirit that transcends any kind of humanly crafted unity.

GOD'S GLORY IN THE CHURCH TODAY

Now that we have a better idea of what God's glory is and how it brings unity, let's look at some of the exciting things that are happening in the body of Christ today that are moving us quickly into a level of unity that has not been experienced since the first century A.D. Through the ministry of the Holy Spirit God is revealing and sharing His glory with His people.

THE GOLD AND THE GLORY

One of the greatest symbols of glory is gold. If God's glory is the means to unity, then God is announcing an increase in the release of His glory to prepare us for greater unity, through the numerous manifestations of gold dust, tooth fillings and crowns and other such things. From Argentina to Toronto; from Anaheim to South Korea; thousands of Christians have experienced first hand God's glory through the miraculous manifestations of gold.

I have personally seen several miracle gold fillings and crowns. Numerous ministers of the gospel, such as Ché Ahn of Anaheim, California, and John Arnott of Toronto, Ontario, have been blessed with an anointing to release gold fillings and crowns to people in their services.

Even more people have had gold dust appear on their body and clothes. One young lady, who recently attended a meeting where gold dust was manifesting in abundance, came to one of our meetings with a significant amount of gold dust between the pages of her Bible. She poured out some into my wife's Bible, where it now sparkles on the pages where it was poured. We will not try to prove or provide extensive documentation about this phenomenon in this book, but I believe that those who are seeking greater verification will find it in many other sources.

This golden manifestation of God's glory is a sign and a wonder that points people to the fact that God is releasing His glory on earth. To those who receive gold fillings or crowns it is also a very practical and awesome blessing. But each one who experiences this manifestation firsthand, and each one who hears their testimonies, is made to focus on the Giver of gold, the One who gives us the power to gain wealth. And when the focus is on Him, it is not on ourselves and our greatness, but on Him and His grace, mercy and glory.

EMPHASIS ON INTIMACY

Wave after wave of teaching with accompanying testimonies on the subject of intimacy have been sweeping over many modern day Christian movements and churches. From young children and teens to silver-haired intercessors, many hungry souls have been entering into a dimension of spiritual experience that was extremely rare a decade or two ago.

Many have been raised up to teach others to cry out for a deeper personal relationship through their awe-inspiring testimonies. Heidi Baker, an amazing missionary to Mozambique, who has had many Heavenly encounters, cries out in her conferences, "Is anyone here hungry for fresh bread?" Or, "Is there anyone here who wants more of Jesus?" The result is that hundreds of eager North American church folk and non-church folk race to the front, in hopes of finding a place in the large auditorium to prostrate themselves on the floor to seek the Lord.

Todd Bentley, a young man in his twenties, talks about His experiences in intimate dreams, visions and Heavenly experiences. He shares how he was so desperate that he would spend six to twelve hours or so every day for several months just praying, waiting and seeking God. Now he teaches incredible truths from the Word of God about such things as "Open Heavens" and "The Secret Place."

Shawn Bolz, another prophetic brother, still in his twenties at this writing, shares about his trips to the "Throne Room," where God revealed many exciting things to him, some of which are too sacred to share at this point. While driving his car between two cities in Missouri, he was transported into the presence of God. He was then suddenly back on the road, but already at his destination city, hours before he should have arrived at normal highway speed. A similar experience happened on his way back home. His experiences have come after years of prophetic preparation of seeking God and laying down his life for the Lord. At times he suffered rejection and injustice. Other times he experienced extreme demonic attacks. But everywhere God leads him to share today, young people and old alike are pressing into the intimate presence of God and thousands of lives have been changed in a very short period of time since these and other powerful experiences.

Mike Bickle, whom God has chosen to head up a huge international youth movement out of Kansas City, Missouri, has had his calling confirmed twice hearing the audible voice of God. He has encouraged multiplied tens of thousands of Christians to move into a life of prayer and fasting to prepare for a huge youth-led revival which has been prophesied by Paul Cain and others. International Houses of Prayer are being raised up throughout the earth. It is one of the fastest growing movements in Christianity today.

The interesting thing is that God gave Mike Bickle the assignment of studying and imparting to others the Old Testament book, "The Song of Solomon." This was not a natural fit for him, being the son of a world champion boxer. His focus had been on other things, but God has called him to focus on the "bridal" paradigm and his ministry in Kansas City goes by the name, "Friends of the Bridegroom." His constant focus with all the prayer and fasting is intimacy with God.

Other men like the prophet, Bob Jones, have been having heavenly visitations for years. Some have remarked that "Bob goes to Heaven as routinely as most of us go to Walmart." During his many years of prophetic ministry he has developed an intimacy with God that is remarkable, but not as rare today as it used to be.

The list of men and women, who have tasted of the glory of God goes on and on. Men like Rick Joyner, who has had amazing visions and revelations. Women like Jill Austin, Patricia King and Stacey Campbell, to name a few, have been drawn up into the heavenly realm in one level or another. Many of them have seen and experienced the glory of God as Moses and Paul did in other eras.

Again we come to the application of all this information. The glory of God was given to the church to produce unity. Studying doctrine can sometimes unite and sometimes divide, but those who see and experience a manifestation of the glory of God have an awesome proactive unity amongst them. They are all in love with the same Lord Jesus, and they all want to see His glory again and again. Their focus is on Him and not themselves or their brothers and sisters. They worship more intensely and experience more intimacy. They bring the love they received from God to their world and share it with everyone they meet.

Hearing the stories from these spiritual "trailblazers" into the heavenlies creates a hunger and a thirst in us who hear them. It awakens our inner longing to know Him. It has been there all the time, but we have tried to satisfy it with so many other things. Other voices have drowned out His still small voice. Other sights have bombarded us in our fast moving society, so that we have not noticed how little time we have taken to look upon His face and behold Him in His glory and beauty. In these intensely significant days of history, we are being reminded that He is preparing His return trip to the earth as the "Magnificent Bridegroom" and He is now preparing His beautiful bride.

THE RAM AND THE MOUNTAIN OF THE LORD

At a recent conference we attended in Red Deer, Alberta, Canada, there was a strong emphasis on unity. During worship I saw a brief vision of the Mountain of the Lord, with His glory covering the top of the mountain. My eyes focused on a majestic ram, who was leading the sheep up the mountain into the presence of God.

The ram was standing still with his head turned, looking back at the sheep who were following him. I looked into his eyes and saw amazing strength, passion and love towards his sheep. I knew that the ram represented the Lord. Then I heard His heart say, "I want eye contact with my sheep."

Without looking back at the sheep, I perceived that they were not keeping their eyes on Him like they should. Some were afraid of stumbling on the loose rocks in their journey up the mountain. They I remembered the Scripture, "I will guide you with my eye" (Psalm 32:8). I knew that if the sheep would keep eye contact with their Leader, He would protect them and warn them, speaking to them with His most expressive eyes.

I felt later that some of the sheep were not so fearful, but rather distracted with many things on their journey. Some loved to look around at the other sheep and point out their faults and their imperfect features. They would compare themselves among themselves and try to look better than others in the eyes of their peers.

Meanwhile, the Ram was waiting for them to look His way. He wanted eye contact. I so remember when Brenda and I were courting. Sometimes we would just look into each other's eyes, without saying anything for a few moments. Somehow, we could talk with our eyes and know what the other was saying. That is how it is with our Heavenly Bridegroom. He wants to speak to us with His eyes. He wants intimacy of the deepest kind. We must not rob Him of that. He paid too high a price for that intimacy.

Lest anyone think the Ram is a strange representation of Jesus, remember the ram caught in the thicket that became the substitute sacrifice for Isaac. Abraham offered up that ram in place of his son. Jesus became the fulfillment of that prophetic act, and was sacrificed for us in our place.

Those who keep looking up to their Leader, who give Him the eye contact that He desires, will find themselves moving quickly up into the mountain of the Lord and into more and more of His awesome glory. And the quicker we partake of more of His glory, the quicker we will find ourselves in a position of unity with others who are partaking of that same glory.

MOUNTAIN OF THE LORD WITH MANY PATHWAYS

Earlier, in a prayer meeting in Dallas, Texas, I had received another little vision of the Mountain of the Lord. In this vision, I saw a large mountain at its base. I knew it represented the pathway to the glory of God. People were coming towards this mountain from every direction, wanting to find God and to experience His presence. These were not people who just wanted religion. Scribes and Pharisees and hypocrites were not included. These were the true seekers of God, who wanted to know God in Spirit and in truth.

These people came in groups of all sizes. Some represented whole movements or denominations. Some represented different social and ethnic groups and nationalities. Each group started to make a pathway up the mountain, by winding their way around it because it was a very steep slope, too steep to take straight up. Because the mountain was wide as well as high, there was a lot of room for people groups to make their own pathway and keep pretty much to themselves.

But as they moved higher up the mountain, I saw something unexpected taking place. Since the mountain was getting narrower, there was not as much room for separate pathways anymore. I saw two pathways merging into one. The people on the pathway began to visit with each other and discovered that they had the same goals and desires and they truly loved the same King of Glory. More and more pathways began to merge as they approached the cloud of glory at the top of the mountain.

The final scene was the whole group holding hands in a huge circle around the King of Kings and Lord of Lords. They were all worshipping in total unity, totally focused on the object of their symphonious worship.

The obvious conclusion was that the closer we get to the glory of God, the more unity we will experience with other sincere seekers of His glory.

MORE INSIGHT ON HOW HIS GLORY PRODUCES UNITY

Since writing the above insights on unity and the glory given us by Jesus, some fresh revelation has been coming that has added much to my own understanding of this strategic truth. I found a virtual gold mine in II Corinthians 3, which has become a very special chapter to me. I had preached on the final verses before, but never with as much enthusiasm and passion as I do today.

This awesome chapter lays the foundation in the first few verses and then builds a beautiful truth which is climaxed in the final verse – a verse which is very familiar, but seldom understood in its full meaning. The basic truth in this chapter is that we have been given an awesome dose of God's glory, and as we become aware of it, we are changed and transformed into His image.

Paul begins the chapter with some basic declarations:

1. The saints at Corinth are epistles of Christ.

2. Paul wrote on them, not with ink, but by the Spirit of the living God.

3. Writing was not on stone, but on tablets of flesh – their hearts.

4. God makes us sufficient to be ministers of the New Covenant.

5. New covenant is not of letter, but of Spirit. Letter kills, but Spirit gives life.

6. Old covenant was called "Ministry of Death."

7. "Ministry of Death" was so glorious that Moses face shone with God's glory.

8. Glory was fading, but was still so bright that Moses had to wear a veil.

9. New Covenant glory must be much more glorious.

10. New Covenant is the "glory that excels".

11. The veil still exists for unbelievers.

12. Those who turn to the Lord have the veil removed.

After these basic declarations, we come to the capstone of these foundational statements. Here are the final two verses of II Corinthians 3:

"Now the Lord is that Spirit, and where the Spirit of the Lord is, there is liberty. But we all with unveiled face, beholding as in a mirror the glory of the Lord, are being transformed into the same image from glory to glory, just as by the Spirit of the Lord."

The Lord Jesus is that Spirit. Did He not say He was one with God and His Spirit? And where the Spirit of the Lord is, there is liberty. He had already declared that the Spirit gives life, whereas the law brought death. The Spirit was the minister of life in the New Covenant, and the Spirit of God produced "The GLO in the GLORY." Life is not truly life without liberty. God's glory given to us by His Spirit, also gives us freedom from fear of men and freedom from slavery to sin.

God's Spirit gives us the freedom to behold the glory of God without the veil over our face. But notice with me what I have missed for several decades of ministry.

We see His glory when we look in a mirror. We are not looking into Heaven, we are looking at our own faces. How amazing is that!

Are we really supposed to look in a mirror and see God's glory? The resounding answer from the Spirit of God is, "YES!" Now stay with me as we reveal how this is a powerful secret to unity.

First of all, what causes disunity. Proverbs 13:10 (KJV) declares, "Only by pride comes contention." Most of our disunity relates to pride, which often manifests through insecurity.

Built into our humanity is a need for the glory of God to make us special and fulfilled. In the beginning, God made man in His own image. God is a carrier and the Source of all glory. We are not the source, but we were created to be carriers, like Him. When we are not aware of His glory on us and in us, or when we have not accessed the glory that is available to us, **we tend to seek our own glory** to make our inner man complete. But seeking our own glory puts us into competition with others, who also are seeking their own glory.

This problem is just as real in the church world as it is in the secular world. Climbing the ladder of success to fulfill our need for that illusive inner satisfaction or "glory" is happening all the time in both worlds. Just ask anyone who has been involved in church leadership!

Here then is the glorious solution and another window of illumination on the subject of how God's glory makes us one. Remember that Jesus said that He had already given His disciples His glory. Then He sent His Holy Spirit to inhabit His disciples, who became His apostles, filling them to overflowing with His glory.

This glory was upon them all. It first manifested in "cloven tongues of fire." Then it manifested through their "speaking in other tongues." Then it manifested in powerful anointed preaching, accompanied by awesome signs and wonders, with thousands responding to the whole glorious package by repentance and conversion to faith in Jesus Christ.

When these apostles looked at themselves and at each other, they knew, just like the Sanhedrin, that they themselves were uneducated men, but they had been with Jesus, and they had absorbed the glory of Jesus. Centuries earlier, Moses had absorbed

God's glory on the mountain. Like objects that absorb the light and shine for a little while in the dark after the lights are turned out, Moses absorbed the "GLO" of the glory of God. The disciples, like Moses, knew that nothing miraculous was being done by them, but that God's glory was upon them all.

Peter carried the glory of God when he passed by the crowds at the side of the street. They were looking for his shadow to touch them, but more likely, it was the atmosphere of God's glory that touched them as Peter passed by them.

In the early Acts church, there was no longer any competition among them, because they loved Jesus so much and they could see Him in themselves and in each other. Seeing the anointing on each other and on themselves, whom they knew were, by nature, sinful creatures, they were very much aware of the power of God's transforming glory. He was changing them into His own image, by the power of His Spirit upon them.

It was such an awesome time! We know that they were in one accord, because we are told so five times in the first five chapters. That unity came because they were able to see God's glory in themselves and in each other. Their focus was on Him, because He is all they saw. They couldn't see their old nature. They didn't see the flesh. When they looked at themselves and at each other they saw Jesus in His glory, and they were in awe of Him.

In these awesome days, God is restoring the revelation of His glory in His church and in each one of us individually. We need to look often in a mirror and say, "God's glory is in me and on me and flowing out through me. I'm going to see manifestations of His glory working through me to bless others today. I will give Him all the glory for the glory He has placed on my life."

The more we become aware of His glory on us, the more secure we will be in who we are. If we know we have "the glory that excels," we won't need so much of our own glory, the glory that comes through the flesh or through keeping the law. If we see God's glory in others, we won't compare our glory with their glory, because it all comes from God and we give Him the glory. Competition is eliminated. God and His glory become our delight and desire. When we see His glory on others or on ourselves, we see Him and worship Him for who He is.

To make this really sink in, let's remind ourselves as to what this word "glory" means. First of all it means honor. We all want to be honored, but we have received the honor that is given to Jesus, Himself. He has given us His own honor. Why should we seek the honor of men, when we already have the same honor that the Father bestowed on Jesus.

Glory also means "radiant beauty." We look at ourselves and wish we had more natural beauty, but when His glory is seen on us, nobody sees our natural beauty, because they are so taken aback by the radiant beauty of the Risen One, who shines through us in awesome splendor. I have seen my wife many times with this glory on her. It matters not how she sees herself in the flesh, because I have seen her with the glow of God's glory, as she ministers to people. It absolutely redefines the word "beauty" and takes it to a whole new level.

And glory also means greatness, including power, fame and wealth. These are things men seek for, but when it sinks in that we already have all these in the gift of God that has been placed upon us, we just have to live in that confidence and we will experience a level of greatness that we could never accomplish with all the effort we could possibly put into seeking for it. Paul was a top notch Pharisee, through hard work and dedication and zeal. But we would never have remembered him, had he not encountered God's glory on the Damascus Road. That glory came upon him and now we know him as one of the greatest and most powerful and influential leaders of all time.

HELPING OTHERS UNDERSTAND
GOD'S GLORY IN THEM

One of the most powerful ways of restoring the awareness of God's glory in people is through personal prophecy. Since this has been a big part of our ministry, we have seen many people become aware of their purpose and destiny through prophecy. So many have come alive to God as never before, and have rapidly matured into glorious ministers of the gospel. You can often clearly see the "GLO" of the GLORY on their faces.

Western Christianity, as a whole, has revived the skeleton of the Old Covenant, a covenant of works, producing death, rather than life. The saints see themselves as "sinners, just barely saved by grace." They are very much aware of their failures, but not at all aware of the glory that Jesus has given them. They feel too unworthy to be called to "ministry," and pray for the rapture to come before they totally fall away from God and miss it because of their sinful nature.

When we prophesy destiny and vision and hope to people, they often weep, releasing pent up emotions of unworthiness and shame. We repeatedly speak guilt and condemnation off of people who have been enslaved by these cruel masters. As a result, many precious saints have blossomed into radiant servants of Christ, aglow with His glory. In fact, we can say that we have seen them "changed into His image, from glory to glory."

We don't have to prophesy like Isaiah, or Peter, or Cindy Jacobs or Paul Cain to cover someone with God's glory. We can simply say, "God loves you so much, and I feel His love for you flowing right through me." We can say, "I just know deep down inside of me that God has a very special plan for your life, and you haven't missed it. It's still there for you."

We can demonstrate in many practical ways, as well, the love of Jesus. We can give time, energy and finances to reveal God's heart for people. We can write letters to encourage, we can compliment their character and achievements. In all these things we are covering them with glory. After all, if they love Jesus, they are living stones in His temple. Those stones need to be covered with pure gold, a symbol of God's glory.

If we can see God's glory in our mirror and watch it increase, and if we can see God's glory in others and help it to increase, we will be so focused on God and His glory, that there will be no need to seek our own glory. We will all be focused on Him and His glory and He will once again have a people who are His and not their own.

His church will be a people who will radiate the beauty of eternity in the here and now, to prepare all nations for the climax of the ages – the glorious event where Jesus receives His full inheritance in the saints. This is what He has been waiting for. He will have His beautiful bride, full of His own glory, and the honeymoon will last for eternity. This is one story that is not fiction where it will be truthfully said, "They lived happily ever after."

ACCESSING THE GLORY

The message of the glory of God on His people has been coming in almost continuous revelation. Even as II Corinthians 3:18 says we are changed into His image from "glory to glory," so the message of the glory has come to me in a series of partial revelations. Since writing the preceding section of this chapter I was given a further insight which has come in at least three installments.

I knew that we have God's glory available to us and that we should clothe ourselves and others with His glory whenever possible, but I still was wondering if there weren't some more keys to accessing that glory in a more tangible way. We need it to be a little less theoretical and a little more practical.

During a worship service, I was reminded that the two people whose face shone with God's glory had climbed a mountain to be with God. Jesus often climbed a mountain to be alone with His Father. He may have been glowing each time, but we do know that when He took Peter, James and John with Him, His face shone like the sun. We also know that Moses was on Mount Sinai forty days and nights when he saw God's glory and came down with the bright glow on His face.

There had to be something about climbing a mountain that positioned them to receive God's glory. The first truths that came to mind were that when you climbed a mountain, you were not only going uphill and exerting greater energy than walking in the valley, but you were leaving behind many things that make up our normal lives.

At the top of the mountain, you will seldom find a fast food restaurant or buffet. You won't find your friends hanging out there. You won't find places of entertainment. You won't even find employment or business opportunities. The top of the mountain may be a peaceful place, but it is also a lonely place as far as natural company is concerned.

A person who goes on a mountain top pilgrimage leaves almost every possession and comfort behind. He climbs the mountain because he wants something more than all those things. While natural mountain climbers may climb for bragging rights or just because the mountain is there and challenging them, those who climb the mountain of the Lord are climbing it because they believe He is there and that He will meet with them if they leave everything behind to seek Him.

We climb the mountain of the Lord to find something we can't find in the hustle and bustle of the valley. We climb the mountain because there is an emptiness in all the eating and drinking and making merry. We are crying out for something to fill that longing in our souls. What we are crying out for is that mysterious substance that we call the glory of God.

THE MOUNTAINS OF SACRIFICE

Sometime after I was given the first revelation about the mountains climbed by Moses and Jesus, I was reminded on two separate occasions of two other mountains. I will relate them in reverse order to the order in which I received them.

Abraham climbed a mountain with a troubled but faithful heart. He had been asked to give his son to Jehovah as a human sacrifice. It must have been the hardest thing he had ever done, but He wanted to please God and had been given a promise concerning Isaac. God had spoken that He would make of Isaac a mighty nation. So how would that happen if Isaac was killed as a sacrifice? Abraham was wise enough to know it was God's problem. He knew that to please God, He had to believe and obey. Abraham wanted that relationship with God more than he wanted to protect His son.

Of course, God interrupted the sacrifice and provided the ram in Isaac's place, but Abraham's willingness to obey resulted in the greatest glory ever bestowed on him. Listen to the words of the Lord God, in response to the faithfulness of Abraham, His friend:

"By myself I have sworn, says the Lord, because you have done this thing, and have not withheld your son, your only son, in blessing I will bless you, and in multiplying I will multiply your descendents as the stars of the heaven and as the sand of the seashore; and your descendants shall possess the gate of their enemies. In your seed all the nations of the earth shall be blessed, because you have obeyed my voice." *(Genesis 22:16-18)*

Abraham accessed more of God's glory on the mountain of sacrifice than at any other time in his life. This was the honor type of glory and the promise of greatness, including power and influence and prosperity. We don't read about a glow on his face, but it wouldn't surprise me if his countenance was shining like a one thousand watt bulb, after that encounter with the living God.

Abraham's mountain of sacrifice was a prophetic type and shadow of the final mountain climbed by Jesus before He ascended into the presence of His Father. At the top of Mount Calvary Jesus laid down His life. He certainly left every comfort behind and felt every kind of pain imaginable of both soul and body, as He bled and died for our redemption.

I believe the greatest revelation about accessing the glory of God can be seen in this unusual "mountain-top experience." If we really want all of God that He has for us, we also must take up our own cross, whatever that might be in our present situation, and we must climb the mountain of sacrifice and lay down our lives and die.

To get what we cannot lose, we must give up what we cannot keep. We can not take our pride to Heaven with us. There is no place for it. There is no place for selfishness, fear or jealousy. There is no place for criticism, lust or bitterness. There is only room for Jesus. We are found in Him and He is found in us. Nothing of the flesh can go with us into Heaven. We may as well die to it now and be filled with Jesus now.

What we will get in exchange for giving up our own pride, selfishness, greed, etc., is similar to what Jesus got as a reward for His death on Mount Calvary. In Philippians 2, Paul begins with an exhortation to unity. He asks them to fulfill his joy. In our language, we might say, "Make my day!" The way the Philippians could make his day was by using the resources of God's love and compassion and the fellowship of the Holy Spirit to just get along and be in unity.

Paul goes on in the chapter to challenge them to have the mind or attitude of Jesus, who was equal with God in Heaven, but made Himself, "of no reputation." First, He humbled himself to become a man. He allowed Himself to be born in a barn, and ultimately, to be rejected, tortured and abused in every possible way, before He finally breathed His last breath on the cross.

But then we read the following words:

"Therefore God also has highly exalted Him and given Him the name which is above every name, that at the name of Jesus every knee should bow, of those in heaven, and of those on earth, and of those under the earth, and that every tongue should confess that Jesus Christ is Lord, to the glory of God the Father." (Philippians 9-11)

This was the greatest, the ultimate in accessing God's glory. This was honor of the highest order. Because Jesus gave up His own reputation, God gave Him the reputation that would exceed that of any other. The mention of His name would require that all men and creatures everywhere would have to bow the knee and confess that He was their Lord and Master. Notice that while Jesus is receiving the honor of this confession that the glory is going to God, the Father.

This is an awesome illustration of what to do with the glory we receive. When we are honored, we can simply redirect the glory to God, who alone is worthy of honor, glory and praise. He in turn sees that He can trust us with honor and glory and gives us more, which ultimately brings more glory to Himself.

As we stated earlier, if we follow Christ's example and have His attitude, we will be willing to humble ourselves and die to our flesh on the "Mountain of Sacrifice." Then the Lord will begin to show us the glory that we have accessed on His mountain. He will allow honor to come our way. If we make ourselves of no reputation, He will cause our name to be spoken with honor and respect. To be sure, our enemy will stir up some to disgrace us, but we will ignore his attacks and rejoice in the knowledge that we please God and know Him.

DYING AND INTIMACY

The greatest glory that can come to us is to be considered a "special friend" of the most important person around. That is exactly what happens when we take up our cross and climb the "Mountain of Sacrifice" to meet with Jesus and to die to our flesh, so that we can have more of Him.

The result of this pursuit is an opening up of our soul and spirit to the Living Spirit of the Living God. He begins to move upon us with healing balm. He begins to speak to us about how much He loves us and what great things He has prepared for us. He also begins to take us into His confidence about His plans and purposes on the earth as well as in Heaven. He opens up the secret chambers of His heart and draws us into the vast expanse of His passions and desires.

There is no greater expression of intimacy than when one allows another into the secret areas of his or her heart. When God opens up His heart to us, we will experience an ecstasy in intimacy that is unrivaled in any earthly relationship. It starts with dying, but ends up with "unspeakable joy."

A SIGN AND A WONDER

A few months before I began to receive this message, I had seen a quick vision of myself sitting on the floor with a pile of gold coins in front of me. I believe the fact that I was sitting on the floor was symbolic of the fact that I had grown up in relative poverty, although I would not have considered myself poor, just "not rich." Not only had I grown up poor, we had ministered sacrificially in a very poor, even a "welfare mentality" community for many years.

We pioneered a Christian church and non-tuition school as an evangelistic outreach into the community. Both Brenda and I had worked on the side to keep things solvent. Even then, we could not always pay all of our medical and dental bills on time. We never had any extra money for non-essentials. We were not into jewelry or stocks and bonds, etc.

As I noticed the pile of gold in front of me, a stream of gold came out of the pile towards me and covered me with the gold coins. That was the end of the vision and I shared it with Brenda sometime later, when a prophetic word of financial blessing came through someone else.

About a year before this, a pastor of a church in a southwest suburb of Chicago had prophesied over us. He first saw a "brand spanking new motor home." Then he said, "Where is all this money coming from? I see large amounts of money coming to you."

Indeed, God had been blessing financially, and we had been digging ourselves out of debt that had accumulated through our many years of pastoring and two years of transition with very little income. But our motor home was wearing out and threatening to cost us much in repairs, since we had no warranty left on it. We also had a negative equity on our motor home loan. In other words, we still owed significantly more than it was worth. A motor home is not like a house that usually gains equity. It almost always loses equity rapidly, especially when one puts as many miles on it as we do.

So we still had debt and we still had nothing for a down payment on a new motor home. We felt we needed a diesel pusher to handle the work that we gave it, crossing mountain ranges on regular occasions. Also, our boys were getting older and the old motor home was getting too small. Many friends were praying and prophesying blessings and the motor home of our dreams, but it still hadn't happened, and no bank would make us a deal.

But early in the year of this writing, a friend of ours passed away. She and her husband had sold jewelry at a flea market in Chicago for twenty years. After her passing, her husband closed the business and all her accounts. He decided to send us a portion of all her accounts. Suddenly, we were receiving deposits in our account in the amount of several thousand dollars each. Within a few weeks we had received over twenty thousand dollars. Meanwhile, we were still ministering in homes and churches and God was supplying income from these sources as well.

The first thing we did was pay off some of our debts. Meanwhile, our checking account was growing past our immediate needs and we began again to visit RV dealers to see what kinds of deals were available. To make a long story short, through a series of miracles we were able to finance a larger, stronger and more practical motor home.

But God wasn't finished yet. He had just given me the message on how His glory brings us unity, and He wanted to make Brenda and me a sign and a wonder. I had just preached the message on the glory of God making us one for just the second time. The next day we visited the man who had given us the down payment for our motor home.

When we arrived, he pulled out tray after tray of jewelry. Some of it he insisted we take, since he was giving it to a number of charities and he wanted us to have his best. He also asked us to take anything we liked. This was very hard for Brenda, because she was never into jewelry and she didn't want to look greedy. But soon we were being loaded down with more gold, the symbol of God's glory, and precious stones of all kinds.

He turned to me and said, "I don't have much for men, but here's a couple of rings." One was a wedding band with three little diamonds. It replaced the plain pawn shop version we had purchased after my original band had been stolen while playing basketball at a Young Men's Christian Association (YMCA). The other ring had a single, slightly larger diamond. It went on my right hand, where I had never worn anything before. Actually, I had never worn any jewelry of any kind besides my wedding band.

Next, my friend handed me a watch. I had never paid more than $39.00 for a watch. I liked practical watches with many uses. I had been given an expensive watch before, but had given it away to my son, who is a pastor in Spokane, and gone back to my Walmart specials. But this watch, which looked pretty normal was not an ordinary watch. It was a Rolex, with eighteen carat gold.

A little later it occurred to me that I was being covered with gold like never before. God was making us a sign and a wonder to illustrate the message of His glory being poured out on us. Since choosing to serve God with all our hearts and giving up our home life to live a nomadic lifestyle, we have had to die to many things. We are still learning to die, but God has already begun to really demonstrate to us the glory that He bestows on those who climb the "Mountain of Sacrifice."

Brenda has had so much fun with the treasures that had been put in her hands. She has given away literally thousands of dollars worth of women's jewelry, one piece at a time. Many have gone to women in ministry, including pastor's wives, who could never have afforded them. Others went to whomever the Lord would lay on Brenda's heart.

Many times Brenda would wear a ring that she liked to a meeting and then give it away during the meeting, because the Holy Spirit told her to. So many people have been touched by the spreading of God's glory in this way. Many ladies wept openly. Some were given their birthstone, without Brenda knowing what it was. Usually she gave the ring or whatever with an encouraging word that made it even more meaningful.

Our friend returned a couple of times to add a few more treasures so that Brenda could have some more fun giving them away and spreading the glory of God. On the last trip he brought with him the original wedding ring that he had bought for his wife when they were married. It is a ring worth more than my Rolex watch. It was hard for her to accept and not what she had ever wanted, but she wears it as a testimony to the blessings that come when you climb the "Mountain of Sacrifice."

The things of this world really mean very little to us, and we willingly give away anything that God asks us to. Brenda was asked not to give away the wedding ring, but any other possession is just given to us to steward for the Kingdom of God. We have only so much time to build the Kingdom before we graduate from this realm and we don't want any natural possession to take our focus off of the call of God.

There was one other very personal sign from God to confirm this message of God's glory residing on us, but it is something that I am not free to write about at this time. But it totally completed the picture for me that God's glory is on His children, and if we want it we can have it. We carry as much of God's glory as we really want. Personally, I am not satisfied in the least with the level of glory that exudes from my being. I am motivated to climb that mountain and access more and more of Him.

CHAPTER 5

THERE IS ONE BODY

MY PERSONAL REVIVAL

*A*s a freshman in Bible College, before I entered the seminary program in Regina, Saskatchewan, Canada, I had a time of visitation from God. I shared parts of this experience in my first little book, "Heal Your Body, Lord." This was such a life-transforming experience that I must share it here also.

I was the third surviving son of very zealous Pentecostal parents, who had come out of the Mennonite church before I was born, because they had embraced Pentecostal beliefs. They had lived by faith as missionaries in Northern British Colombia, after not being allowed to go to Africa, because of health reasons. Both my brother Dave, who has been a full-time missionary in Latin America for three decades, and I, were born on that mission field.

I had grown up loving God and wanting to serve Him. I had a considerable battle with youthful temptations, but never even considered laying down the call of God for the pleasures of this world. As a child, I had read through the Bible several times before I reached my teens. By the end of high school I had memorized close to a thousand verses. I did enjoy the attention I got winning contests in Bible Clubs and Vacation Bible Schools, etc. In short, I was a straight and sometimes self-righteous kid. I was separated from the world in most areas of life and was loving Bible School. I enjoyed every class as well as the social life. I was still struggling with moral issues, but was determined to serve God with all my heart.

Then one evening, I took part in a required dorm prayer meeting, which happened about once a month. Eight of us young men met in our dorm room. One of the seniors led the prayer meeting and asked us if we had any burdens. What he meant was that we needed some prayer requests to pray for. Most people had unsaved loved ones or someone sick or needy in some way. That was what the leader was asking for. But God used his words like a sharp sword to pierce my heart.

As soon as I heard the words, "Does anyone have a burden?" the Holy Spirit spoke to me, "You don't have any." And I knew it was true. I loved God and was enjoying Bible School, but I really wasn't carrying any burdens for others in intercessory prayer. My whole family was saved and in good health. I didn't have many unsaved friends and I was quite happy with my life. I knew that God's heart was aching for the lost and that we should be carrying the burdens on His heart with him. I was convicted!

Suddenly, I had a burden, but not the kind that would make me look good or "spiritual." When my turn came to speak up, I had to either make something up or be honest. I had been raised very strictly to be honest to a fault, and when I was asked for my burden, I answered, "My burden is that I don't have one." I was not trying to be "cute." I had no other option and I humbly confessed that I lacked the heart of God for souls, etc.

I had absolutely no idea how much this one simple act of humbling myself would radically revolutionize my whole life. I thought I should have a burden for lost souls, but the burden that God placed upon my heart was not the normal concern for unsaved family and friends. Instead God began to reveal His heart for His church, the body of His Son, Jesus, on the earth.

Almost overnight, God gave me a passion for revival in His church. I didn't have the revelation of the body then that I now have, but I knew that on the front burner of His heart was His desire to restore His church to its former glory. My burdens were not so much for individuals as they were for the whole church or body of Christ. I quickly was made aware of the fact that if we could fix the church, we would see many souls saved and the harvest would be brought in by God's powerful harvest machine – the church.

I began to rise early every morning to have time to spend with the Lord and His word. The book of Acts came alive to me and I would read about one half of it every day. Having a Pentecostal background, I liked to pray out loud and cry out to God. I couldn't do that in my dorm room. So every morning, I made my way from my dorm room about 5:30 to the administration building where the cafeteria and the piano practice rooms were located on the bottom floor, below the classrooms and chapel. The little practice room, where I practiced my voice lessons, became my prayer closet.

Most of my prayer time was spent on my knees with my Bible on the piano bench. Every time I would read about the early church in the book of Acts, my heart was broken afresh with the burden of the Lord for His church. I would cry out to God, "Revive your church. Your church is a sleeping giant! Wake us up, Lord! You haven't changed, we have. We've lost so much and don't even know it." At that point in my theological training, I didn't know anything about "Restoration Theology," which states that the church is in the process of being restored to its original state of unity and power. All I knew was that the church that I had experienced in my short life had little resemblance to the church that I was reading about in the book of Acts.

After crying out and shedding many tears for an hour or two, sometimes right through the breakfast hour, the burden would lift and an incredible joy would flood my soul. I would go through the rest of the day with a tremendous peace and love for everyone.

FRINGE BENEFITS OF CARRYING HIS BURDENS

1. Fruit of the Holy Spirit

I quickly discovered that there were significant benefits to carrying the burden of the Lord. The first was the wonderful flow of the fruit of the Spirit – Love, Joy and Peace and also longsuffering, faith, etc. They came without effort. They just flowed from the overflow or afterglow of being in His presence. I could love my roommate when he was angry at me for no reason. I had the joy of the Lord no matter what the circumstances were and I was at peace with my classmates and professors and even my roommate. He ultimately let me know how much he respected me and how much I had changed.

It's interesting that I was burdened for the restoration of the gifts of the Holy Spirit, but the first thing that I received was the fruit of the Spirit. I really wasn't manifesting many of the gifts at that time. I believe that those who seek the gifts for the right motives, that is, to expand and proclaim the Kingdom of God, will also be blessed with the fruit of the Holy Spirit.

2. Moral Freedom

The second benefit was a new and complete freedom from the moral bondage which I had been fighting for several years. I'm not sure when it hit me, but sooner or later I realized that I had not had to wrestle with this issue since I began interceding for revival for the church. The only thing I had done to get the victory was to become a burden bearer for the Kingdom of God. This victory was another source of joy and inner peace.

3. Brenda

The third awesome benefit of this personal revival was that God brought a lovely young lady, named Brenda Pinkerton, into my life after this revival had been going on for a month or two. She had not been taught much about the Holy Spirit or spiritual gifts but she had a deep hunger for more of God.

I had been studying the subject of prayer and was writing a paper on "Praying in the Holy Ghost" in a Christian and Missionary Alliance college. I was so excited about the concept of the power of prayer and spiritual gifts and I was full to overflowing. In a very real sense, I'm sure there was a degree of the glory of God on me during those days. I'm sure what Brenda saw in me was that glow from the fire of God within me as well as a strange and revolutionary faith that God would do great miracles in the church again.

At any rate she was an outlet for my zeal for God and prayer and she soaked it up like a sponge. She still loves to soak in God's presence and teaches the concept of soaking in the presence of God so that you have something to give out to others. Soon God was speaking to me about her in my prayer times. He was telling me that He had prepared her for me and me for her. Ultimately, it worked out that way, and our unusual romance (our dates were Bible studies) has turned into an unusual ministry life together.

REVIVAL PRAYER ANSWERED – INSTALLMENT # 1

Believe it or not, this whole story relates to the subject of the body of Christ. Please stay with me while I connect the dots.

The intercessory prayers that I had been praying were mostly for revival. I had read about many, but had never seen one. But God didn't have me pray and intercede just for my personal benefit. He was preparing to bring revival to our city and our region. Just a few years later, a revival team came to our city, Regina, after spending eight exciting weeks in Saskatoon, a city north of Regina.

The revival team held their first Regina meeting in the chapel, right above the little piano practice room where I had prayed so earnestly for revival for several months. I was probably the first one to the altar, knowing I needed a fresh touch from God. I had gotten so busy that I had lost that freshness of sweet communion with Him that I had known before. I was not only married and still in seminary, but I also was pastoring a country church in Parry, Saskatchewan, and working another job part time on the side. I was already burning out in my mid-twenties, and needed revival myself.

The revival meetings moved to a large church and continued for six solid weeks, going well past midnight most of the time. People were meeting God in repentance and restoration of relationships. A great unity and love flowed among the hundreds of people who gathered night after night. It was not everything I had dreamed about, because there were not a lot of physical miracles, or conversions, but it was at least a step in the right direction. Christians were recognizing their need for more of God and were crying out for His power in their lives.

REVIVAL PRAYER ANSWERED – INSTALLMENT #2

It wasn't long though until I was invited by my older evangelist friend, Elmer Burnette to accompany him to Argentina. Brenda knew right away that God wanted me to go and she released me, even though we had never been separated for more than a day or two. This was a six week trip and would be the most awesome and exciting experience that I have had in my entire life.

It was the fall of 1973. Brenda was pregnant with our second child and went to stay with her family in Seattle. I journeyed south to Albany, Oregon, where I joined Pastor Burnette. Together we flew to Cordoba, Argentina, where we were met by almost one hundred worshipping Christians, singing "Hallelujah" from the balcony of the airport. It was the only song they knew that we could understand.

Our first meeting in a relatively small church was blessed by two awesome miracles. A lady was healed of breast cancer and the pastor's son was healed of a crooked spine. In addition, before the healings occurred, there was a powerful spirit of repentance released after Pastor Burnette preached an anointed message from Psalm 51.

The next night we were in a large auditorium. The Spirit of revival in the atmosphere was powerful. Pastors who hadn't spoken to each other were asking each other for forgiveness and embracing in public and then sitting together on the large platform. The Spirit of unity was the preparation for the Spirit of revival. Then the people began to worship. It was a style of worship we had never experienced. People were totally lost in the presence of God. They sang the same chorus over and over, while they swayed and danced and waved their hands before the Lord. After about an hour of heavenly worship, my mentor, Brother Burnette (as we called him), began to speak through a Spanish interpreter.

THE GLORY CLOUD

Before getting very deep into his message, Brother Burnette noticed what appeared to be a cloud of smoke coming in through the large open doors at the back of the auditorium. He immediately asked Jack Schissler, our missionary host, about it. But Jack didn't see anything. Brother Burnette realized that he was seeing a glory cloud and waited on God for direction. The cloud moved to the front of the crowd and hovered over the right side of the room. A small cloud dropped down from the larger cloud, and in the cloud he saw the number nine. He heard the word arthritis in his spirit, and asked, "Are there nine people with arthritis in this front section?" Nine people in the section raised their hands.

The cloud moved quickly to another section and another number appeared. Soon all the folk who had raised their hands were at the altar receiving prayer from pastors and Bible School students. There was a lot of excitement as a number of people began to experience immediate healing. Before the group at the front could be encouraged to take their seats, Brother Burnette was getting more revelation and people with hearing problems or vision problems or heart problems, etc. were quickly brought up to receive prayer, while the first group was encouraged to take their seats.

MIRACLES PRODUCE DESIRED RESULTS

After two or three hours of ministry and numerous miracles, Brother Burnette would say to the crowd, "You have seen Jesus do all these miracles. How many of you want this Jesus to come into your life and be your Savior?" Every night 15-50 people would respond to the salvation invitation. When these folk had been ministered to at the altar, he would ask, "How many of you want to be filled with the same Holy Spirit that has been working here tonight?" A large group would come forward every night and receive ministry to be filled with the Holy Spirit.

I had never been in such an atmosphere. It was the closest thing I had ever seen to what I had read about in the book of Acts. The love was so thick and powerful that you could feel it in the air. Affectionate greetings in Latin American style were so richly felt that you felt loved from head to toe. Miracles were happening every day and the excitement was so great, that it seemed the whole city was buzzing with anticipation for the next meeting.

GIFTS OR FRUIT?

I had heard preachers in the past declaring that the fruit of the Holy Spirit was more important than the gifts. They had focused on love and how important it was that we love one another. But what I observed is that even though they were talking about love, neither they nor the people that heard their messages were very good at practicing love to the extent that people really felt that they were loved. I often felt the opposite coming from them while they argued that we shouldn't focus on miracles and signs and wonders.

But in this setting, where the gifts of the Holy Spirit were flowing like a river, so was an awesomely real and penetrating love. It was truly not the love of man, but a genuine flow from the Holy Spirit, Himself. It isn't an either/or situation where we choose either the gifts of the Spirit or the fruit of the Spirit. Rather, it is the gifts of the Spirit producing the fruit of the Spirit and the fruit of the Spirit producing more gifts of the Spirit.

Eight years earlier I had been so excited about the gifts of the Holy Spirit that I prayed with many tears for them to be restored to the church. The immediate result had been the presence of the fruit of the Holy Spirit. I felt more love, joy and peace than ever before. Now we were seeing the manifestation of those desired gifts and the result was the same – more manifestations of the fruit of the Holy Spirit.

THE BODY VISION

After almost six weeks of "Heaven on Earth," in several Argentine cities, with meetings usually twice a day, Brother Burnette was asked to minister to leaders in daytime sessions. In the two major cities where we had held extended meetings, he shared some of his personal testimony and gave a challenge to the leaders. Then he made himself available to them for personal ministry. One by one or as couples they came for prayer.

For each person who came to him, God would immediately give him a vision of the person's life. He knew nothing about the leaders and workers, but the missionary knew them all and confirmed the incredible accuracy of every word. I don't remember any of them not being broken and weeping before God. It was an awesome time, and I began to desire him to do the same for me, even though I was his assistant on the trip. I reasoned that it would be better if I waited until he could minister to Brenda and me together, but the desire just increased. Finally, I asked him to pray for me. This was what he saw.

First, he saw a little crippled child, which he affirmed was me, trying to put two little twigs together in the shape of a cross. My body was so deformed and twisted that I couldn't do it and I was crying. A group of people were standing to the side and watching me and they were crying, too.

As he watched, he saw different parts of my body being healed and straightening out. One member of my body after another began to take the proper form and shape and soon I had two larger sticks and was making a cross with them. As my body continued to heal and to grow, soon I was putting larger boards together and making a bigger cross. Finally, there was a large cross and I was standing in the shadows, worshipping the Lord. The people on the side were raising their hands and worshiping with me.

The truth of this vision really pierced to the core of my heart, just like the word about not having a burden had done years before. I knew that although I may have looked good to people, as a pastor and husband and father, I had lost much of my passion for God and for His church. I had been rewarded for my earlier passion with this awesome time in Argentina, but I would be going back to my responsibilities in Canada, where I had been really too busy to seek intimacy with God on a regular basis.

I knew that I didn't look as good to God as I did to others. It was like when Ezekiel was given God's eyes to see the Valley of Dry Bones in Ezekiel 37. These were the living Israelites, that looked normal to everyone else, but God saw them as very dry skeletons. They looked alive to man, but dead to God.

I know that I am covered with the righteousness of God in Christ, but God was showing me the level of my effectiveness with what He had already given me. I was not moving the hearts of men by the power of the Spirit of God. I was preaching well thought out truths, based on personal study and Seminary training. The people liked my preaching and they liked us, but I had lost my passion for change. I was too content with the status quo. All that was about to change!

As Brother Burnette shared the vision as he was seeing it, I began to explode with weeping and sobbing, like I had never experienced before. I saw my failure and weakness, but also His grace and mercy to heal me and restore me and give me the high calling of presenting the message of the cross and all its power.

A FAVORITE AUNT

When we returned to our room at the missionary's house, Brother Burnette asked me about the appearance of an aunt that I had talked about, who had been very special in my life while I was growing up. He had noticed one person in particular, who had stood out in the vision in the crowd of people watching me. He described her well, but I had no photos of her with me to verify that she was the one he had seen.

Later, on our journey home, we stopped for several meetings in Colombia, South America, where my brother, Dave and his wife, Arlene, were missionaries. One morning I noticed their wedding album on the coffee table. I looked through the album looking for my aunt's picture. She was not in any of their wedding pictures, but inside the back cover, there was another photo, which was of the wedding of our older brother, Fred, and his wife, Marty. Since my aunt had gotten them together and was a best friend of Marty, she had been a bridesmaid or "Matron of Honor," and therefore in the wedding party photo.

I closed the album and waited for Pastor Burnette to rise for breakfast. He went straight to the album and asked me, "Is your aunt in this album?" I believe he already knew by revelation. I acknowledged that she was and he leafed through every page until he got to the back cover. He pointed her out and said, "That's the lady I saw in your vision in Argentina."

Later, when I brought him to Regina, where my aunt lived, I introduced them to each other. Brother Burnette greeted her, "I saw you in Argentina last fall. Only your hair was longer then." "That's right," she responded, "I just had it cut recently."

I share all these details to provide credibility to this whole story, because this story is not really so much about me as it is about the heart of God for His whole church. Until a few years ago, I did not realize the larger significance of that vision, but now I understand it to be a "Job Description" for my life and ministry.

FROM MY BODY TO HIS BODY

The body that was broken and deformed not only represented me, but the whole body of Christ on the earth. There are thousands of church organizations and para-church organizations around the world, all trying to present the message of the cross to individuals and to the masses. But our efforts have been so feeble and power-less, compared to that of the early church. We have done what we have been taught to do in our institutions of higher learning, but the results have been less than the effort gone into them.

God has given me a charge to bring healing to His body. It's the body that Jesus, the Christ, or "Anointed One," has to work with on this earth. When we started traveling, I wrote my first small book, which I titled, "Heal Your Body, Lord." I've often said that it is the most important book I'll ever write. The exception may be this book, which covers the same basic subject of unity, with an expanded revelation of God's purpose and plan for bringing His whole body into unity. It's interesting that my first and my seventh book are on the same subject. God does like the number seven a lot! But of course, His favorite is still the number one.

For too long the church has considered the "Body of Christ" to be a metaphor, a figure of speech to help us understand the function of the church. But the Bible clearly declares in many places that WE ARE THE BODY OF CHRIST! We are not a picture of the body, and we are not like a body, but we **ARE** the body of Christ. We are His hands, feet and mouth to do His work on the earth.

I'd like now to quote an edited version from "Heal Your Body, Lord." This edited version was written immediately following the release of the incredible blockbuster movie, "The Passion of the Christ."

THE FATHER'S PASSION AND PLAN FOR THE BODY OF JESUS

The intensity of Jesus' suffering and death have never been more clearly understood than they are today, except for those who actually witnessed it 2000 years ago. Mel Gibson's "The Passion of the Christ" has given our society a new depth of understanding of His pain and agony. It has given us a new appreciation of His love and sacrifice for us.

But what about the Father, who loved us enough to let His only begotten Son face such incredible pain and lay down His life for us. Let's consider what the Father endured watching Jesus absorb the agony and the violence inflicted on Him by those who hated Him with a passion. It was only because He knew that there was no other way to bring about the necessary result, that He was able to endure watching His Son experience what He did.

The Father had given to His own precious Son a strong healthy body that did everything required of it. The body of Jesus walked, talked, and reached out to touch and heal. But now, on the cross, that body, just like the bread its hands had broken into pieces and distributed to His disciples, was itself being broken by men inspired by the evil one who hated what that body was doing on the earth. They wanted to kill that body and destroy its ability to heal the sick, raise the dead and set captives free. And so the Father watched in great pain as that divine creation, Jesus' body, was being mutilated until it could function as a body no more.

The Father in His eternal wisdom and foreknowledge had already determined what to do. He would recreate and resurrect that body on the third day. It would be more marvelous and powerful than its earlier counterpart. With that post-resurrection body, Jesus came and went, appearing and vanishing at will. After completing His mission on earth, the Son returned to the Father's side where He was received and exalted and given a name, which is above every name.

But the story doesn't end there. The Father then authorized His Son to send the same Holy Spirit, which had inhabited His old earthly body, back to the earth to inhabit a much larger body. This body would simply replace the body that His Son had used earlier on the earth.

Once again, the Father looked at the marvelous creation which He had brought into being. Once again the body was functioning with all its members fulfilling their purpose and calling. The results were awesome, and were recorded in the book of Acts. The body was exactly what He had intended it to be. And God may have looked at this new creation, like He did in Genesis, and said to Himself, "I did good!"

But soon little germs, viruses and bacteria were attacking the body in various places. At first, the body successfully dealt with these intruders, but little by little, some of them began to take hold. Then the body, while still accomplishing amazing things, began to come under more and more internal and external attacks. Some of these attacks only strengthened the body, but others began to take their toll. Bruises, sores, diseases and bone fractures left it severely hampered in its effectiveness.

Like the original body of the Christ on the cross, life was slipping away until it seemed that there was no life left at all. Looking at this new body in the "dark ages" reminds us of Isaiah 53:2, which tells us, "there was no beauty in Him that we should desire Him." Until the time of the Reformation, which was the beginning of the Restoration of the church, there was almost no reason for anyone to desire Him in that body on the earth. It was twisted, deformed and diseased.

But once again, the Father had a magnificent plan to resurrect and restore the body of His beloved Son on the earth. Once again this body would become more awesome in power and glorious in the functioning of every part than its predecessor in the book of Acts. This awesome body, now spread out over the face of the globe has the fantastic potential to radically change the face of modern society world-wide, and to reveal the glory of the Father more than the early church ever did. We are now entering the third day, the third millennium since the birth of the Christ Child in Bethlehem, and on this third day we are seeing the glorious resurrection of the Magnificent Christ in His own awesome and glorious body.

Once again, the Father can look down at His creation and say, "I did good!" And this new body that He has created for His own awesome Son will never again be subject to the spiritual diseases and afflictions of this world. It will remain awesome and strong, even when under attack of all kinds. It will reflect the beauty and glory of the One who resides by His Holy Spirit within it. The earth will once again flock to wherever this body is serving the needs of the people. Blind eyes will be opened, deaf ears will hear, the lame will leap for joy, the cancers will disappear, the AIDS patients will be healed and every affliction and bondage known to man will lose its power to steal, kill and destroy human life.

And the most glorious result will be that souls will be saved by the millions and hundreds of millions. The gospel of the Kingdom, the good news that THE KING has taken His throne and will establish a rule and reign of righteousness on the earth, will go out to all the people groups of every nation with signs following, so that the harvest will be quick and glorious.

We have seen "The Passion of The Christ!" Get ready now for "The Resurrection of His Body."

A PERSONAL VISION

In the summer of 2002, we were attending a wonderful camp/conference in Sylvan Lake, Alberta, where a local ministry had put together a great team of ministries. One night, after the preaching, a lot of ministry was going on at the altar and I found myself on the floor, with people praying all around me. I began to ask God for a glimpse of Him and His glory. I was praying for spiritual vision to see what my natural eyes could not see.

Soon I was seeing a sheet drop down from Heaven, like the one Peter had seen filled with unclean animals. The sheet was empty, but I was being invited to get on it to be lifted up into Heaven. I joke now that I was the "unclean animal" that was getting on the sheet. The whole vision, including the "sheet" part was very unclear and foggy gray. I couldn't see anything clearly, but I could see something approaching me. I kept praying for the scales to be taken off my eyes, but everything stayed that same foggy gray.

Finally, I began to make out what it was that was approaching me. It was a person in a wheel chair, and I knew it was the Lord, in His earthly body. I know it is not how He appears to others in Glory, but it was a reminder for me of the message He has given me to preach concerning the restoration of His body on the earth. Again, I was brought to tears and weeping over His body. It is a message I must preach, and I can't talk about too many subjects in the Kingdom of God without speaking about unity and the healing of His body.

HEALTHY BODY = POTENTIAL FOR GREAT PRODUCTIVITY

So many people question why the church lacks the power of the early church. To me the answer is simple. The early church was a whole and healthy body of Christ, in tune with the Head. Today's church is, for the most part, segmented, crippled and out of touch with the Head. You can't expect an unhealthy and deformed body, with many of its members not aware of their function, to produce much for God.

On the other hand, as we see healing coming to the body and unity increasing daily, we can look forward with excitement to some great and awesome days ahead. The world has yet to see the explosive power of signs and wonders on a world-wide scale, but it is truly coming in our generation. Every day we find more and more humble hearts that want only to see God's glory, rather than establish themselves as people who should be honored and praised for their great spiritual gifts and anointings. We are tremendously encouraged about the future.

THE PROBLEM OF EVIL SOLVED

Theologians and pastors have struggled with explaining the problem of evil for centuries. People ask why there is so much suffering in the world, if God is good and all powerful. He could have surely made life easier for us all. We know that the devil is involved, but He could also have prevented him from having the power that he enjoys.

There are some special situations, such as God bringing judgments on a sinful nation, or God allowing saints to earn a greater resurrection (Hebrews 11:35), but the basic answer to the question is that the problem of evil is not God's fault or problem, it is ours, the church, in which He has delegated His power to reverse evil on the earth.

You see, when Jesus walked on the earth and something evil had happened, He reversed the evil. If a storm was about to overturn the ship, Jesus commanded the storm to cease. If there was a shortage of wine for the wedding, Jesus turned water into wine. If someone died prematurely, He raised him from the dead. If a person was blind or diseased or demonized, He simply made them whole. When we were in sin, He died an awful death to reverse the effect of sin. Jesus' whole life and death was about reversing the problem of evil in His world.

The early church, His new body, did the same on an even larger scale. While the church was still in unity, tremendous miracles were taking place, healing all that were sick and tormented by evil spirits and even raising the dead. Once again, evil could not prevail in the presence of the true church of the Risen Christ. Today, the church is spread out into most of the populated world, but we are mostly powerless to stop the pain of evil around us. I believe the reason is simply that we are too selfish and proud to get together with the rest of the body of Christ and pray for wisdom and understanding to bring healing back to the body of Christ for His sake and His glory.

Again, I rejoice that this is now happening, and we, the church, the one and only body of Christ, the anointed One, on the earth, will see God's power released more and more to reverse the problems of evil that are occurring all around us. I believe that more and more prophetic people will be activated in predicting and preventing disasters from occurring, including terrorist attacks. I do believe this is already happening. There are some very high level prophets that have had access to presidents and other world leaders, speaking into their lives on a fairly regular basis. This should increase greatly in this decade and in the decades to come.

May God accelerate the healing process of His own body, for His own honor and His own glory!

Chapter 6

ONE BODY, ONE BREAD

A very simple revelation about the body of Christ came to me through a passage relating to communion in I Corinthians 10. The passage reads like this:

> *"The cup of blessing which we bless, is it not the communion of the blood of Christ?" The bread which we break, is it not the communion of the body of Christ? For we, being many, are one bread and one body; for we all partake of that one bread." (I Cor. 10:16, 17)*

The word communion in the above passage means sharing. So the cup we drink is the sharing of His blood and the bread we break is the sharing of His body. And we, being many are **one bread** and **one body**, for we all partake of that one bread.

We already know that the bread represent His body, so what is there to learn from these two verses and their context? And what does it have to do with our subject of unity? It's really very simple, yet quite profound.

We are often told that we are the "one body" of Christ, but this may be the only Scripture that tells us that we are also the "one bread." Because we partake of His body, which was broken for us, we together become one bread, just as we together become one body.

The key to understanding this revelation is to keep reading through I Corinthians 12. Here Paul talks about spiritual gifts and then goes on to talk about the fact that we are all members of the body. The gifts, obviously, give us our function in that body. We are also informed that each member is important and that we must not be jealous of each other, but rather, we must do what God has gifted us to do. It is also clear from studying this chapter that no one can do it all. We don't possess all the gifts to use them whenever we desire.

GET THE PICTURE

This then is the picture that I see. When Jesus broke the bread and divided it up among the disciples, the bread represented His body, which they were soon to become. He would give each of them a piece of the bread, which represented a part or function of His body, as described in I Corinthians 12. One was the eye, another the ear, another the nose, etc. If they brought their gifts together and used them in unity of purpose, the body would be a whole and healthy body that would accomplish much in the earth. But if the parts of the body did not come together in unity, the body would be weak and unable to accomplish its intended purpose.

As the pieces of broken bread represented various gifts and ministry, which the Father had given to Jesus without measure or limitation, so the bread would not be a complete loaf, if they didn't come together with their portions. A broken piece of bread is rough looking and has jagged edges, which represents us trying to be something with our gift, outside the body of Christ. But if you put those broken pieces back together again, you can just see one beautiful golden brown loaf once again.

I have illustrated this truth when serving communion. With the right kind of "kosher" communion bread, you can put pieces back together in such a way that you can't see that they were ever broken. That is how we are to be in unity with each other. No one should see even a little crack between us, because we fit together so well, just the way Jesus intended us to.

USING OUR GIFTS

True unity is not the absence of division. It is actually working together for one common goal, with one common heart. Unity is not just getting along for a couple of hours on Sunday with those we really don't know that well. Unity is serving God side by side with those we know very well, as well as those we don't know so well, using our various gifts, even when our gifts flow in different styles and anointings.

We all have different ideas of what is the best method and the proper way to use our gifts. We are sure that our ideas are better than our co-workers, and wish they would listen to us and do things our way. That's where we know if we have the spirit of unity or not. Do we remind ourselves that Jesus prayed, "I pray that they all may be ONE?" Or do we think that He said, "I pray that they all may be RIGHT?"

Regardless of how well we feel that we flow together with others, it is extremely important that we determine that we will develop and use our gifts for His glory and the rapid expansion of His Kingdom, while there is still time and opportunity to do so. The night comes when no man can work. And we must use His tools, if we hope to get His projects completed.

None of man's ways and means will get His job done. God knows what needs to be done and He has provided the tools to get the job done. Those tools are the spiritual gifts that give us our function and position in the body of Christ. We must learn how to use them with grace and skill and we must learn to do so and stay in harmony with those that we work with.

HUMILITY – THE KEY TO HARMONY

The secret is humility. Proverbs 13:10 says, "Only by pride comes contention." (KJV). It's not our different ideas that divide us; it's our pride in our ideas. We so love to be right. We so NEED to be right! But we need to get over it, and instead desire to be ONE rather than RIGHT. We need to listen to each other, and we need to hear each other's hearts. We will find that many of our differences are just from seeing the same thing from a different perspective.

In recent years, God has brought so many leaders together that have never come together before. They have joined together in strategic round table discussions, in conferences and seminars, where they have learned from each other and expanded their own understanding of the "present truths" that God is reviving in His church today. The result is that people from many different ecclesiastical backgrounds are coming together to hear ministries that they would have never listened to before. The leaders are paving the way for their people, and the whole church of Jesus is coming together in a unity that hasn't happened since the early church.

THE BODY AND THE BLOOD

Getting back to the original scripture in I Corinthians 10:16, 17, we need to understand the symbolism a little better. Jesus was saying more than we see on the surface. There is something more than what we have learned in the past about bread and wine, and how they represent the body and blood that can teach us valuable truths regarding unity and harmony in the church today.

THE CUP

The cup of wine, which Paul said is the "sharing" of the blood of Christ, was just one cup. They did not have separate sterile cups to drink from. They all drank from the same cup. The wine or grape juice, whichever it was, (It's the same word in the Greek.) was dark and red like blood, and was filled with nutrients for a healthy body. The blood flowing through our bodies reaches every cell in our bodies, bearing nutrients and oxygen to them.

The life is in the blood, according to Leviticus 17:11. The blood carries life to all the parts of the body. This, to me, represents the ministry of the Holy Spirit, who brings the life of Jesus to all parts of the body of Christ. We are told, "There is one body and one Spirit." (Ephesians 4:4). Just as they drank from one cup, we receive life from one Spirit. And we all partake of that same Holy Spirit.

But for the blood to properly flow through the body, the body needs to be connected. If my arm is separated from the body, it's going to have a problem getting the life blood to it to keep it alive. Instead, the blood it already has will drain from the body and it will lose all signs of life. Separated from the body of Christ, we lose the life of the Holy Spirit, represented by the cup, which was shared by all the disciples. But when we are together, in one accord, like the early Acts church, we find the Holy Spirit working through us all and bringing life to each member of the body.

THE BREAD

Jesus referred to Himself in John 6:35 as the Bread of Life. Bread was the staple of life in Jesus' day. Whole wheat bread, as it was made in those days, contains most of the necessary nutrients for life and health. People could literally live on bread and water. That's why Jesus said He was both the Bread of Life and the Living Water. We can live on Him. He is everything we really need.

When Jesus broke the bread at communion, He didn't serve separate packaged pieces of bread or cracker. It's a lot more convenient for larger churches today, but it doesn't really portray what Jesus was teaching. Jesus took one loaf and divided it up, so each one could have a part. He was giving Himself to them, dividing up His ministries and giftings, so that all His disciples would have the health and strength to fulfill their roles and functions in His body.

SHARING

The key word in this Scripture is the word "communion," which means "sharing." We must realize that none of us have a corner on a truth, or a gift, or a ministry. We all are given a part of the ministry of Jesus, but we are sharing it with others. The life of our gift or function is even dependent on our relationship with others. We share from the same cup, the same Spirit of Life. And we share one loaf of bread, but together we are "one loaf."

I cannot understand communion just by thinking of the sacrifice that Jesus made for me as an individual sinner. I must understand that in order to be a player on His team, I must have real living relationships with others who have received the same Spirit of Life and have partaken of the same Bread of Life. He has imparted His gifts and ministries to all of us.

This understanding does not minimize the traditional understanding of communion as a remembrance of the suffering and death of Jesus for us. In fact, it should increase our appreciation of what He has done for us. He not only gave us our salvation through His death and resurrection, but He has also given us His POWER, through the spiritual gifts that He has blessed us with.

We now not only remember what He did for us, but now we do for others what He did when He walked among men. We preach the gospel of the Kingdom, proclaiming Jesus as our King. We heal the sick with His power. We set captives free from demonic power and in His name we also have authority to even raise the dead.

It is all represented in that "sharing" of His body, which is our bread, and in the "sharing" of His blood, which is the Life we receive from His Holy Spirit. That Life flowed through His veins, and now flows through the veins of His new body on the earth. That body is you and I and all other souls who have received His salvation.

SPIRITUAL GIFTS AND THE BODY

The various lists of ministries and spiritual gifts in the New Testament all are simply ministries and gifts of Jesus. He manifests Himself through His gifts. Let's look at how that works.

ROMANS 12

The list in Romans 12 is often called "Motivational Gifts." They are prophesying, serving, teaching, exhortation, giving, leading and showing mercy. These gifts are all expressions of the desires from the heart of God, which Jesus carried with Him, being empowered by the Holy Spirit.

Whenever we use these gifts to serve, speak for God, show mercy, lead or give, etc., we are the body of Jesus in action.

I CORINTHIANS 12

This list has been dubbed, "Manifestation Gifts," because they are called manifestations of the Holy Spirit. But they are also manifestations of Jesus in our midst. They include three categories.

The first is the **Mind of Christ** revealed through words of Knowledge, Wisdom and Discerning of Spirits. The second is the **Voice of Jesus** through the gifts of Prophecy, Tongues and Interpretation of Tongues. The third is the **Power of Jesus** through the gifts of Faith, Healings and Miracles.

Through these gifts, Jesus speaks, touches and reveals His mind, just as if He were still with us in person. These gifts were used continuously by the apostles in the "Early Acts" church. The results were that people heard from Jesus and were touched by Him in beautiful ways. Ananias and Sapphira also discovered that

Jesus knew their secrets and that He would not allow sin to go undetected in His virgin church.

EPHESIANS 4

These gifts have been titled, "Ministry Gifts." They are Apostles, Prophets, Evangelists, Pastors and Teachers. Through the Apostles, Jesus governs, casts vision, administrates and leads the church. Through the Prophets, Jesus speaks to apostles, evangelists, pastors and teachers and every saint in the body of Christ.

Through Evangelists, Jesus goes to the ends of the earth, revealing the awesome message of the cross and redemption. Through Pastors, Jesus loves, heals and nourishes the sheep and lambs who have been brought into the fold. Through Teachers, Jesus reveals His nuggets of truths to those who are hungry for His revelation.

These three sets of gifts, plus a different arrangement of gifts near the end of I Corinthians 12, all are expressions of Jesus, who is living among us through His gifts. Is it any wonder that the enemy wants to tell us that these gifts are not for today. Without these gifts operating freely, Jesus cannot be what He wants to be or do what He wants to do in the church which is His body, which He has purchased with His own blood.

CHAPTER 7

A PROPHETIC PICTURE OF UNITY

*T*he book of I Chronicles has captured my attention recently as a pattern for how God prepares us for the coming of His glory. The awesome glory of God came and filled the temple in II Chronicles, but most of the preparation for that glory came in the events of the book of I Chronicles.

I see ten major prophetic pictures in the pages of I Chronicles.

1. The People Had a Clear Understanding of Family Relationships.

Most of the first several chapters of I Chronicles are filled with genealogies. Not exciting reading material to most folk. But what struck me was that everyone knew who his father was and everyone knew who his children were. They took pains to keep track of who they belonged to and who belonged to them.

God is preparing us for an outpouring of His glory by letting us know that He truly wants to be a Father to us, and He is revealing what an awesome Father that He really is. Not only that, we are finding that He is giving us earthly relationships with those who are spiritual fathers and spiritual children. And we are finding out who they are. It's like the storybook scenario, where parents and children have been separated and then discover who they are and meet after years or decades of separation.

God wants us to know our family tree and have the security of knowing that there are those who will always be there for us and those who need us to be there for them. When we know who we are and who our Father is and who our children are, we have a place of security on that level, which will actually free us to desire more on a different level.

2. There Was a Holy Dissatisfaction with Present Possessions

In I Chronicles 4:9,10, we have the now famous "Prayer of Jabez." He had the security of knowing who he was, but was not satisfied with his lot in life. He knew that his life had already caused pain and he wanted to be fulfilled by being a blessing. He cried out to the Lord for an expansion of his territory and a blessing from God. Jabez knew that if he had more of God and His blessings, He could then give more of God and be more of a blessing. If Jabez had had no sense of identity and didn't know to whom he belonged, his life would have been focused on that issue instead of focusing on his next area of need.

God's glory seldom falls without someone crying out for it. Moses was privileged to see God's glory after he asked God earnestly for it. If we are insecure in our basic identity we won't be focused on asking God to reveal His glory. God created us to be dissatisfied with everything but the fullness of His presence in complete intimacy and unity with Him.

On the other hand, if we get set in our ways and lose our hunger, being satisfied while we are in a state of being incomplete, because we have gotten used to it, we will likely never taste the new wine or see the greater glory of God. Being content with the earthly comforts that we have is a good thing, as Paul taught us in I Timothy 6, but being satisfied with what we have in spiritual things is not a good thing. Jesus said, "Blessed are those who hunger and thirst for righteousness, for they shall be filled." (Matthew 5:6)

3. Tabernacle Gatekeepers Were in Position

I Chronicles 9:17-27 gives us the story of the tabernacle gatekeepers in David's day. I believe there is much prophetic symbolism in these eleven verses, but to me verse 27 is the most significant. It says that the gatekeepers lodged around the tabernacle and every morning they opened the doors to the House of God.

We are living in a new millennium. It is truly the beginning of a new day. It is the dawning of the third "Millennial Day" since Jesus was here. It is the time for the gatekeepers to open the doors to the House of God and usher people into the presence of the Lord. As the angels rolled away the stone on the third day, it's time for the gatekeepers to open the gates into Heaven. They will allow the glory of God to come down out of Heaven onto His people in this "Third Day" of New Testament history.

Worshippers and "Forerunners," who visit the "invisible" realm are gatekeepers who open doors for us to follow them into the ever-increasing manifestations of the presence of the Living God. God is quickly putting more and more of these in place, facing them in every direction as the gates of the tabernacle did in Jerusalem.

4. Israel Had to Let Go of the Old Order

People had to make a choice. They could hold onto the declining glory of the House of Saul, or they could accept God's anointed replacement, which was the House of David. In Chapter 10 we see the people making that choice and coming to join with David.

We don't let go of tradition very easily. We love our ecclesiastical comfort zones and sacred security blankets. But we can never know

God's best without letting go of the old wineskin to make way for the new wine. Israel quickly blossomed under the anointed leadership of King David. Today the church has a choice. Either we go with the stale and rancid taste of our traditional church structure, or we move on to something more living and fresh and full of the blessing and anointing of Jesus on it.

We are seeing this taking place all over the world. People are being set free of the baggage of religion and men's traditions. People are moving into the Tabernacle of David anointing, and they are entering into a freedom in worship, using spiritual gifts for God's glory. It is not just a small phenomenon; it is a major shaking in the church at large.

5. Warriors From Every Tribe United Under the Anointed King

Now we will look at I Chronicles 12 as a prophetic picture of the unity that is coming on the church to prepare us for the coming of His awesome glory on the earth. It is such an awesome picture of what God is actually doing on the earth today.

In order to make the transition from the House of Saul to the House of David, every tribe sent its mightiest warriors to where David was. The warriors were to represent their tribes and confirm that each tribe was in agreement that they wanted to make David the king over all of Israel. Changes in royalty from one family to another was not a common thing as long as the last king had an heir. It took a show of strength and unity to accomplish this feat.

I encourage every reader to read carefully through I Chronicles 12. The expressions of military skill and valor are so applicable to spiritual warfare. For instance, there were warriors skillful with both spear and shield. They had offensive and defensive weapons. Others were skillful in all kinds of military weapons. They were versatile. Of others it talks about courage, keeping rank and having wisdom to know what Israel ought to do.

The story ends with a great celebration and the statement that all of the people were in unity after the warriors from every tribe had united. It was a time of great joy and gladness, except for perhaps a few from the previous royal family of Saul, who had lost their potential for royal privileges. Note the following comment:

"All these men of war, who could keep ranks, came to Hebron with a loyal heart, to make David king over all Israel; and all the rest of Israel were of one mind to make David king. And they were there with David three days, eating and drinking, for their brethren had prepared for them. Moreover those who were near to them from as far away as Issachar and Zebulun and Naphtali, were bringing food on donkeys and camels, on mules and oxen – provisions of flour and cakes of figs and cakes of raisins, wine and oil and oxen and sheep abundantly, for there was joy in Israel." (I Chronicles 12:38-40)

PROPHETIC APPLICATION OF UNITED WARRIORS

I see the tribes as representing different movements and denominations. I believe that God has warriors, which we would normally call intercessors, in every group. I believe that some have been called to stay in hard, dry places as warriors, fighting for a change in the minds and hearts of the leaders.

These warriors become skilled in battle, because they get a lot of practice in those situations. They come for training to the Lord of Hosts, who teaches their hands to fight and encourages them for the battle. They seem to be getting nowhere for a period of time, but eventually cracks begin to appear in the walls of resistance and they find others who will join them in their spiritual warfare.

Some who join them will be from other tribes and denominations. But they will have the same goal: to replace the present rulers and to make Jesus the true King over their tribe. They fight on knowing that God has already given them the victory.

I believe that the Lord will reward the faithfulness of His mighty warriors with many miracles and changes in their movements. While some will resist and become the enemies of Jesus, many of the resistant tribes will come into agreement with those who want Jesus to have total control of His church.

Because God is strategically placing so many intercessors in unseen places, and because He is increasing their skills and strength in battle, an incredible move towards unity is taking place in all the earth. The warriors in every tribe and denomination are bringing their strength and influence and giving it totally to Jesus, increasing His Kingdom in its rule and reign on the earth.

The result is that we are that much closer to the great and awesome outpouring of God's glory, which will fill His Living Temple. The Gatekeepers are opening the gates and the Warriors are bringing the rest of the people through their prayers.

6. David Brought in the Presence of God

In chapters 13-16 of I Chronicles, we read about the process that David went through to bring the Ark of God to Jerusalem. His first attempt ended in failure, but later He discovered God's pattern and was successful in bringing the Ark into the Tabernacle that he had prepared for it.

We know that God dwells in the praises of His people. He loves for us to worship Him and praise Him for all He has done. But our praises and worship must come from hearts that are sanctified, like the priests who were to carry the Ark. The ox cart that carried the Ark the first time would be like putting it in a pick-up truck today. It's the machine that carries things for us. Perhaps some of our "worship" machines are just mechanical devices that we use to get us from one place to another without fulfilling our calling to carry the presence of God ourselves through sanctified hearts and hands.

At any rate, David learned much about the presence of the Lord and developed worship music, instruments and choirs that alternated in a twenty-four/seven continuous worship. He took worship to its highest level ever. We don't read that God commanded him to do this, but because He was a "man after God's own heart," he knew how much God loved His worship and He wanted all Israel to know the joy of pure worship in His presence.

Learning to bring God's presence into our gatherings and daily living is a requirement and preparation for the coming of the glory of God. We have seen a tremendous increase in the depth and power of corporate and private worship in the last few years. We are certainly in the preparation process for God's glory to fall on us in unprecedented fashion.

7. David Repents of Pride

In chapter 21, we find the story of David sending out Joab to number all the armies of Israel. We know that counting is not a sin, but obviously from the text, even Joab knew that David was indulging himself in a "pride thing." David had been highly exalted and had complete power over all of Israel and also had all neighboring nations under his dominion, after conquering them in battle. He had increased in power and his armies had grown with the expansion of his reign. He just was very curious about how big his armies really were. There was no strategic reason for counting them. He had no fear of attack by this time, and if he were attacked, God was always with him and would give him the victory, no matter what the odds were.

The simple fact is that David wanted to boast about the might of His kingdom. It cost him much and caused many innocent people to die. But David recognized his sin and repented with deep sincerity of heart.

Today, God is calling leaders to search their hearts and purify their motives. There have been jealousies, divisions and strife among leaders, because of a similar type of pride. Proverbs 13:10 declares, "Only by pride comes contention . . ." (KJV).

If we want the glory of God to fall in our midst, we must let go of our ambition to make a name for ourselves and our spirit of competition to do better than another ministry down the street. May God help us to be honest and let go of that stinking flesh that promotes ourselves instead of Jesus and His Kingdom.

As our ministry grows in scope and people honor us in various ways, there is often a subtle voice in my mind that says, "You're really going somewhere. People are recognizing your gifts, etc." I imagine that most people hear similar voices, when they start to become successful. We need to squelch those voices as soon as they come. We need to be on guard against every little root of pride and keep it from growing up and producing a disaster. We need to deflect all the praise to Jesus and thank Him for His mercy and grace that allows us to do anything at all that blesses His Kingdom. In our flesh dwells no good thing, but His grace covers us and enables us to do awesome exploits in His name.

8. David, Representing the Older Generation, Prophesied to Young Solomon

I Chronicles 22 is one of the most powerful Old Testament prophetic types and shadows of the coming glory of God. Please carefully read the following verses.

Now David said, "Solomon my son is young and inexperienced, and the house that is to be built for the Lord must be exceedingly magnificent, famous and glorious throughout all countries. I will now make preparations for it." So David made abundant preparations before his death.

Then he called for his son Solomon, and charged him to build a house for the Lord God of Israel. And David said to

Solomon: "My son, as for me, it was in my mind to build a house to the name of the Lord my God; but the word of the Lord came to me, saying, 'You have shed much blood and have made great wards; you shall not build a house for My name, because you have shed much blood on the earth in My sight.

'Behold, a son shall be born to you, who shall be a man of rest; and I will give him rest from all his enemies all around. His name shall be Solomon, for I will give peace and quietness to Israel in his days. He shall build a house for My name, and he shall be My son, and I will be his Father; and I will establish the throne of his kingdom over Israel forever.'

"Now, my son, may the Lord be with you; and may you prosper, and build the house of the Lord your God, as He has said to you. Only may the Lord give you wisdom and understanding and give you charge concerning Israel, that you may keep the law of the Lord your God. Then you will prosper, if you take care to fulfill the statutes and judgments with which the Lord charged Moses concerning Israel. Be strong and of good courage; do not fear nor be dismayed." (I Chronicles 22:5-13)

In this passage, David reveals his passion for a glorious house to be built that will be famous in every country. He would not tolerate anything mediocre or inferior.

But the point we want to focus on in this section is the fact that David heard from God for his son and prophesied to him what God had given him. The point I see here is that it was the older generation prophesying to the younger generation. He was giving Solomon a very vivid and powerful sense of destiny. This prince of Israel didn't have to wonder what he would be or do in life. He was given that destiny through the prophetic word of a natural and spiritual father.

Today, God is calling for the older generation to release and empower the younger generation, through prophetically speaking destiny into their lives. This is being spoken in many ways through many leaders in the land. And we are seeing it happen. It is happening in places like Kansas City, Missouri, under the International House of Prayer ministry. We are seeing it happen in our ministry in Illinois, and Alberta, Canada, and many other regions. Young people are responding in great numbers to the challenge of building a glorious house for the Lord. They are looking for spiritual fathers to prophesy destiny and purpose into their lives. When they receive these words, they rise up and take their place in the army of the Lord. It is an awesome and glorious sight to behold.

The only house that we want to have a part in preparing for, as part of the older generation, is a house where the former glory of Pentecost has been restored and exceeding in power and magnitude. The "Stadium Vision" of Paul Cain is a prime example of what we want to see take place. It will be a "nameless and faceless" group of young people who will take the glory of God to the stadiums of this nation and the world. Supernatural power, released in signs, wonders and miracles, will be taking place. News reporters will be recording incredible miracles, including the raising of the dead. This move of God and the revelation of His glory will be accelerated, if the older generation fulfills their responsibility to impart vision and destiny to the younger generation.

9. Great and Generous Giving For the House of God Took Place

In Chapter 22 and again in chapter 29 of I Chronicles, David expresses his love for God and His house, by donating huge amounts of gold, silver, precious stones and all types of materials for the temple. The value of the gold alone was in the hundreds of billions of U.S. dollars at today's prices. Note the love expressed in the following verses:

Now for the house of my God I have prepared with all my might; gold for things to be made of gold, silver for things of silver, bronze for things of bronze, iron for things of iron, wood for things of wood, onyx stones, stones to be set, glistening stones of various colors, all kinds of precious stones, and marble slabs in abundance.

Moreover, because I have set my affection on the house of my God, I have given to the house of my God over and above all that I have prepared for the holy house, my own special treasure of gold and silver; (I Chronicles 29:2,3)

David not only gave the wealth of the kingdom for this project, but also some of his own private stash of the very best gold available. It was several billion dollars worth.

David didn't just prophesy to the younger generation. He financed them as well. This is taking place and will take place much more in our day. Even as revealed through Shawn Bolz, God has released his heavenly "Minister of Finance" to put money into the hands of those who have a Kingdom heart, in order to finance the gathering in of the Lord's inheritance, His bride. We have seen the signs in the natural that God is doing that very thing in the supernatural.

Our passion right now as a ministry team is the empowering and financing of the "young and the restless" into their divine destiny. They are quickly getting themselves ready. They may be "young and inexperienced" like Solomon, but they have the faith to believe that God can use them anyway to build His house in every nation on the face of the earth. And God has given us the faith to believe that He wants to let them do just that. Wherever we can, we try to help finance young people to fulfill their calling.

God is calling and empowering business and church leaders to work together to see that a lack of finances is not the reason that the world doesn't hear about the power and love of our Savior and

Lord. Rather, they are determined that the resources of Heaven are going to become the resources on the earth to finance this great harvest time, when God's children everywhere will be gathered together to worship Him.

10. David took Israel to a Higher Level of Worship

Before the glory of God fell in the early chapters of II Chronicles, we find that David placed renewed emphasis on worship.

Moreover David and the captains of the army separated for the service some of the sons of Asaph, of Heman, and of Jeduthun, who should prophesy with harps, stringed instruments, and cymbals. (I Chronicles 25:1)

. . .The sons of Asaph were under the direction of Asaph, who prophesied according to the order of the king. (I Chronicles 25:2)

. . .Of their father Jeduthun, who prophesied with a harp to give thanks and to praise the Lord. (I Chronicles 25:3)

All these were the sons of Heman, the king's seer, in the words of God, to exalt His horn. (I Chronicles 25:5)

So the number of them, with their brethren who were instructed in the songs of the Lord, all who were skillful, was two hundred and eighty-eight. (I Chronicles 25:7)

These specially gifted and talented musicians were not just to show off their talent, but they were to move in a prophetic anointing. Heman was one of the king's seers, or prophets. They were all to be listening to God and playing what He wanted them to play. They were also skilled in the "Songs of the Lord." This we understand to be spontaneous songs sung in worship to the Lord, as well as songs that were prophetic, coming from the heart of God.

God is raising up worship again to realms of the prophetic that we have never seen before. We first heard about the "Song of the

Lord" in the early "eighties." Today, we hear much about "Harp and Bowl" worship and prayer. It is intimate, scripture-based, prophetic and moving. Leaders like Asaph, Heman and Jeduthun, are developing their skills in prophetic worship and training multitudes of others to minister to the Lord and the people in this way.

Truly, we are being taken to a higher level of worship in these days as a preparation for the coming of the glory of God in mighty power.

SUMMARY

This chapter has focused on the preparation for the coming of the glory of God on the earth. But interwoven with that is the concept of unity. From the knowledge of family relationships, to the desire of Jabez to be a blessing, to the dedicated gatekeepers taking their responsibilities, to agreeing together to let go of the old order, to the warriors uniting to make David king, to the learning to bring in the presence of God, to repentance from Pride, to the prophesying to the younger generation, to the generous sacrificial giving and to the coming of prophetic worship in the house of God, unity of the hearts of men was always a crucial ingredient.

But now, let us see the proof-positive that unity was directly involved when the glory of God fell. Read with open eyes and ears the following passage:

Indeed it came to pass, when the trumpeters and singers were as one, to make one sound to be heard in praising and thanking the Lord, and when they lifted up their voices with the trumpets and cymbals and instruments of music, and praised the Lord, saying:

"For He is good, for His mercy endures forever,"

that the house, the house of the Lord, was filled with a cloud, so that the priests could not continue ministering because

of the cloud; for the glory of the Lord filled the house of God.
(II Chronicles 5:13,14)

Even with the awesome worship, it was when they all came
into a unity or "oneness" that the cloud of glory filled the place. All
that happened in the first book of the Chronicles was in preparation
for what happened here in II Chronicles.

The result of this manifestation of God's glory was that Solomon
blessed the people and then prayed a great prayer to God on behalf
of the people. After his prayer, God responded in a powerful way.
Please read the following:

Now when Solomon had finished praying, fire came down
from heaven and consumed the burnt offering and the
sacrifices; and the glory of the Lord filled the temple. And
the priests could not enter the house of the Lord, because
the glory of the Lord had filled the Lords house.

When all the children of Israel saw how the fire came down,
and the glory of the Lord on the temple, they bowed their
faces to the ground on the pavement, and worshipped and
praised the Lord, saying:

"For the Lord is good, for His mercy endures forever."

Then the king and all the people offered sacrifices before the
Lord." (II Chronicles 7:1-4)

Again we see the glory of God falling. This time it comes with
fire consuming the burnt offering. Following this many more
sacrifices were offered to the Lord.

A few verses later we read that God visited Solomon by night
and made a new covenant with him which is often quoted today,
at least in part. It is the famous, "If my people" passage and
promises us healing and restoration when we have gone astray,
if we will only humble ourselves, pray, seek God's face and turn

from our wicked ways. This promise is one that we still need to bring before the Lord for our nations.

Again we have seen that unity brings God on the scene and God on the scene produces more unity. We must pursue that unity through pursuing the glory of God together with others of like mind. The results will be off the charts and out of this world.

CHAPTER 8

UNDERSTANDING THE PATTERN OF DIVISION

*I*f we can learn a little more about our enemy's methods that divide us, we can probably intercept his plans and agenda a little more quickly. We have already seen some of these things in operation, but we will try to get a clearer focus on our enemy's method of operation to keep us from fulfilling our destiny as the church of Jesus Christ, His body on the earth.

1. The enemy robs us of the awareness of the glory which God has given us.

Our enemy uses guilt and condemnation as major tools to break in and steal from us the glory of God, which makes us one. When we feel we are unworthy of His glory and power and love, we must make it on our own. We get competitive, let our pride hang out and offend others. Others do the same to us and it becomes a civil war.

The solution is to receive the truth of God's forgiveness and mercy, and access the glory, as we shared in chapter four. Then we must begin to spread the glory on others. The best way to do that is through prophetic words and through acts of love and kindness to demonstrate God's love and kindness.

2. The enemy exalts the mind over the heart.

God's focus is always on the heart, but the enemy of our soul focuses on the mind and makes it his playground. He puts doubts and questions there that foster confusion or strife. He also makes us think that our ideas are better than others and if everyone would just listen to us, we and/or they would be successful. We develop a pride in "doing it right" or "knowing the truth," and look down on others who don't have the superior knowledge that we have.

The solution is to refocus on the heart; first our own and then others. If God looks on the heart, and we are supposed to be like Him, then we should also. We need to ignore the offenses people give us and focus on the pain in their hearts that causes those offenses to come. Minister healing words and actions to them and watch them change.

3. The enemy helps us become analytical, critical or cynical.

It's easy to get critical or cynical if we first become overly analytical. We try to understand and analyze too much with our natural minds. We see so much phoniness that we tend to look at new things with a cynical or critical spirit. We are so afraid of believing something false that we also reject what is true. I've noticed certain cultures have more problems with this than others. There is an attitude towards politicians and preachers, just like there is toward car salesmen or telemarketers.

The solution is to ask the Lord to soften our hearts and increase the gift of discerning of spirits, so we won't reject the true, for fear of embracing the false.

4. We become building inspectors instead of builders.

This is a follow up of the last point. When we are quick to scrutinize everything that comes our way, we tend to feel that we have a gift of "discerning the cause of every problem" in the church. We become self-appointed "building inspectors." Instead of working harder to build when things go wrong, we join the other "inspectors," who have also laid down their tools and picked up their inspection clipboards to figure out what is wrong.

It's no wonder things grind to a halt when all the builders become inspectors. If they would leave the inspection job to the Holy Spirit and the gifted leaders He has empowered in the church, and begin to build again, by earnest prayer and a ministry of encouragement, the problems would most likely be quickly resolved. The greatest solution to a negative situation is a positive spirit and positive actions.

One of our enemy's tricks is to so consume us with internal strife, that we forget our mandate to bless His people and give good news to the lost. The more we lay our tools down, the more the problems will persist.

5. Success produces pride and independence.

As mentioned earlier, it is so easy to feel good about ourselves and forget our need for God and others. A great hindrance to unity is the independent spirit that says, "I'm a man or woman of God, and I know what I'm doing. I don't need your help or advice. Just leave me alone, and God and I will build His Kingdom." If we could handle success better, we would experience much more, I am sure.

We need to always remember to keep small in our own eyes and give praise and glory to God for every opportunity we have to speak or act on His behalf. The solution to pride is to humble ourselves before God and man, rather than to wait for God to humble us.

6. Bad teaching causes distrust in others.

Someone said, "Bad doctrine is a cruel taskmaster." People with bad doctrines usually emphasize how wrong you are if you don't believe their doctrines. It becomes a vicious circle. We are taught that we are right and others wrong. We are taught to believe that what we believe is so important that we may be the only people who please God and know the truth. The result is that we won't listen to anyone else who could set us free with liberating truths. Naturally, we are suspicious of others who don't believe like we do. We become more and more defensive and more proud of our own beliefs.

The more we are taught to distrust others, the more we should question what we have been taught. If we have the Holy Spirit with us and in us, we can ask Him to help us discern truth and error. We need to be open to other believers who may see things a bit differently. If we open our hearts to their hearts, we may both have the "eyes of our hearts" opened.

WHEN UNITY IS NOT POSSIBLE

I want to close this chapter and this book with a clear statement that there will be times when unity is not possible with all who claim to be Christian believers. Our job is not to unite with everyone, but rather to facilitate true unity whenever God gives us the opportunity.

Jesus Himself found no unity with religious leaders. He openly rebuked them, because He clearly discerned an evil heart. He did not come to attack their doctrines, but He zealously challenged them to repent of their wicked motives and thoughts.

We should really hesitate to judge others as being Pharisees the way Jesus did, unless we have clear revelation and instructions from God. The point is that Jesus could not have come into unity with them. The fact was that Jesus did not consider them to be believers, even though they were religious Jews.

We will encounter people like that, but it would be wisdom to always give them the benefit of the doubt, unless we know that we know that we have heard from God that they are wolves in sheep's clothing, who will not repent. For most of us, it would be safer to share the love of Jesus the best way we know how and to listen to their response and heart. When we have given them opportunity and received a response, we need to hear from God, whether or not we should pursue them further.

Most people are not "Anti-God." They are just confused and cynical. A few supernatural manifestations of the love of God will convince them of the truth and bring them into the fold. Religious leaders and those with political power will be the hardest to bring into a transformed relationship with the Lord.

Those who have exalted themselves and will not humble themselves will have a terrible future, but those who soften and allow God to change their hearts, will be accepted by God and can be brought into a unity with His people. Many times people will test us to prove our sincerity. They will appear to be hostile to the gospel, but are inwardly hoping that we will still love them. Eventually, they will be convinced that God loves them also. But if we don't pass the test, they will remain cynical and not accept God's love.

Ultimately, I believe that all who are truly saved will be brought into a powerful unity. Those who will not unite with God's people in the final hours of this age, will not be saved. They may say they believe, but they are not His children, if they don't recognize Him as Father of all of His children, and join the family of God that He Fathers.

FINAL CONCLUSIONS

We started out with the truth that God's favorite number is ONE. We have seen that His heart has so much more desired unity than His church has. We believe that this is changing quickly and the theme of unity is being discussed, preached and taught in Christian circles all over the world.

The obvious conclusion is that God is preparing us for a great climax to this present age. We are living in such awesome, exciting times. God has given us "forerunners" and "trailblazers," who have experienced the things of God in vivid visitations. They are preparing us to enter into the "glory realm" which they have already experienced.

To follow them into heavenly encounters, we unite our hearts with theirs in a unity of the Spirit, crying out for a greater revelation of Him and His glory. We want to have more of God, so we can give more of God to others.

The more we see God's glory, the less we will focus on ourselves and our differences. The more people who encounter God in His glory, the more unity we will have on the earth. Of course, the more unity we have, the more people will believe that Jesus came from God, partly because of the release of God's miracle power that comes through unity.

While we won't be able to be united with everyone, we can pursue unity as hidden treasure, because it truly is worth more than any jewel on the earth. Unity is so highly valued by Jesus, that He made it the main request in His final prayer before Gethsemane. I have chosen to make it my number one request as well for the Church.

Perhaps the concepts shared in this book have brought you to the same conclusions. If so, I encourage you to share these concepts with others, and if you would, let us know that this book was a blessing to you.

You can learn more about our ministry or communicate with us in the following ways:

Website: www.ohmint.org

E-Mail: benrpeters@juno.com

Mailing address:

Ben and Brenda Peters

Open Heart Ministries

15648 Bombay Blvd.

South Beloit, IL 61080

BEN R. PETERS

*W*ith over 35 years of ministry experience, Ben Peters with his wifie, Brenda, have been called to an international apostolic ministry of equipping and activating others. As founders and directors of Open Heart Ministries, Ben and Brenda have ministered to tens of thousands with teaching and prophetic ministry. The result is that many have been saved, healed and delivered and activated into powerful ministries of their own.

Ben has been given significant insights for the body of Christ and has written eight books in the past five years, since beginning a full-time itinerant ministry. His passions and insights include unity in the body of Christ, accessing the glory of God, five-fold team ministry and signs and wonders for the world-wide harvest.

The Peters not only minister at churches, camps, retreats and conferences, but also host numerous conferences with cutting-edge apostolic and prophetic leaders. They reside now in Northern Illinois with the youngest three of their five children, and travel extensively internationally.

Open Heart Ministries
www.ohmint.org
benrpeters@juno.com
15648 Bombay Blvd.
S. Beloit, IL 61080

Printed in the United States
56831LVS00002B/82-90